# ALTCOIN EDGE: CAPTURING GROWTH BEYOND BITCOIN AND ETHEREUM

Identifying the Next Big Opportunities in Cryptocurrency

Theo Quantum

**Ideal Product Solutions**

# CONTENTS

Title Page
Disclaimer　1
Prologue　11
Chapter 1: The Foundations of Altcoins　17
Chapter 2: The Power of Blockchain Technology　37
Chapter 3: DeFi Altcoins　58
Chapter 4: Gaming and Metaverse Altcoins　76
Chapter 5: Privacy-Focused Altcoins　94
Chapter 6: The Role of Utility Altcoins　113
Chapter 7: Green Altcoins and Sustainability　131
Chapter 8: Institutional Adoption of Altcoins　148
Chapter 9: Evaluating Altcoin Projects　167
Chapter 10: Regulation and Legal Trends　189
Chapter 11: Risks and Challenges in Altcoin Investment　209
Chapter 12: Building a Diversified Altcoin Portfolio　229
Chapter 13: Community and Developer Ecosystems　247

| | |
|---|---|
| Chapter 14: Predicting the Future of Altcoins | 264 |
| Chapter 15: The Altcoin Investor's Playbook | 280 |
| Notes | 302 |
| Index | 309 |

# DISCLAIMER

This book is intended solely for educational and informational purposes and does not constitute financial or investment advice. The information provided here aims to offer a foundational understanding of cryptocurrency, digital currency, and blockchain technology, along with general insights into digital asset markets. It is not meant to recommend or endorse any specific investment strategy, currency, or asset.

Investing in cryptocurrency involves significant risk, and past performance does not indicate future results. Readers should perform due diligence and consult a qualified financial or investment advisor before making investment decisions. The author, publisher, and any affiliates are not responsible for any monetary losses or gains that may result from using the information provided in this book. By continuing to read, you acknowledge that this book is an educational resource only, and any investment choices you make are at your own risk.

## Introduction: The Altcoin Edge

The cryptocurrency revolution is no longer just about Bitcoin and Ethereum. These titans of the crypto world have undeniably paved the way, showing us the power of decentralization and blockchain technology. But as these giants dominate headlines and investment portfolios, a quieter, more thrilling revolution is brewing beneath the surface—one that holds the promise of exponential growth, groundbreaking innovation, and untapped opportunities. Welcome to the world of altcoins, where the potential is as vast as the digital universe.

Suppose Bitcoin is digital gold and Ethereum is the canvas for decentralized applications. In that case, altcoins are the pioneers boldly venturing into uncharted territory, redefining what blockchain can achieve. Altcoins—any cryptocurrency that isn't Bitcoin or Ethereum—are building ecosystems beyond mere transactions. They are the foundation for decentralized finance, the creators of virtual worlds, the champions of privacy, and the architects of sustainable technology. They are solving problems Bitcoin and Ethereum can't, carving out niches, and delivering real-world impact.

*Altcoin Edge: Capturing Growth Beyond Bitcoin and Ethereum* is not just a book. It's your trusted compass in the ever-evolving, dynamic world of altcoins. It's your guide to discovering the next big opportunities in cryptocurrency, empowering you to stay ahead of the curve and seize the moment before it becomes mainstream.

## Understanding Altcoins: A World Of Opportunity

Altcoins are the underdogs of the cryptocurrency world, often overlooked by casual investors enamored with Bitcoin's dominance or Ethereum's ubiquity. However, underestimating altcoins is like ignoring the tech startups of the late 1990s that eventually became Amazon, Google, and Facebook. These lesser-known cryptocurrencies are where the action is—innovative technologies, groundbreaking ideas, and the potential for life-changing returns.

Imagine this: a blockchain that enables instantaneous, feeless microtransactions for millions of users daily. Another is that it serves as the backbone of an entirely decentralized internet, where your data is yours and yours alone. Yet another enables creators to monetize digital art in unimaginable ways just a few years ago. These are not fantasies—they are realities driven by altcoins like Solana, Filecoin, and Tezos.

Altcoins cater to specialized use cases, from creating decentralized finance systems that replace traditional banking to establishing virtual economies in gaming and metaverse platforms. They address Bitcoin and Ethereum's scalability issues, introduce novel consensus mechanisms, and embrace green energy solutions. Altcoins aren't just the next phase of cryptocurrency—they're the architects of the future, shaping the global economy in ways we're only beginning to understand.

## The Growth Beyond Bitcoin And Ethereum

Bitcoin is the pioneer, the digital gold standard that brought blockchain into the spotlight. Ethereum, with its programmable smart contracts, revolutionized what blockchain could achieve. But with fame and widespread adoption come scalability issues, high transaction fees, and energy concerns. While groundbreaking, Bitcoin and Ethereum have limitations. And that's where altcoins shine.

For instance, Ethereum's surge in popularity also brought congested networks and skyrocketing gas fees, making it impractical for smaller transactions or applications needing high throughput. Altcoins like Cardano, Polkadot, and Avalanche have taken up the challenge, offering faster, cheaper, and more energy-efficient solutions. Meanwhile, Solana has emerged as a frontrunner in speed, capable of processing tens of thousands of transactions per second at a fraction of Ethereum's cost.

But altcoins' promise goes far beyond fixing what's broken. They are charting new paths, creating value in industries that Bitcoin and Ethereum barely touch. They power decentralized finance (DeFi), enabling lending, borrowing, and earning yields without intermediaries. They are the backbone of virtual worlds in the metaverse, where digital assets like virtual real estate are bought and sold. They introduce revolutionary privacy features, ensuring anonymity in an increasingly surveilled world.

The crypto market's growth story is not just Bitcoin's

price reaching new highs. It's the explosion of new applications and use cases driven by altcoins that are rapidly gaining traction in finance, technology, gaming, and beyond.

## Why Now Is The Time For Altcoin Investors

Timing is everything, and we are standing at the precipice of the next great wave in cryptocurrency innovation. While Bitcoin and Ethereum remain staples in every crypto investor's portfolio, the outsized returns in recent years have come from altcoins. The time to act is now. From DeFi tokens like Uniswap and Aave to metaverse powerhouses like Decentraland, altcoins have transformed early believers into millionaires.

Consider this: In 2021, Axie Infinity (AXS), a gaming token, surged over 11,000%, turning a modest $1,000 investment into more than $100,000 in less than a year. Solana (SOL), a blockchain designed for high-speed transactions, saw its value skyrocket over 10,000%, becoming a top-10 cryptocurrency. These stories are not anomalies; they prove the staggering potential of altcoins.

Investors who understand the nuances of altcoins —how to identify promising projects, evaluate their potential, and time their investments—stand to capture unparalleled growth opportunities. But success in the altcoin market isn't just about luck. It's about knowledge, strategy, and the ability to separate the hidden gems from the noise.

This is where Altcoin Edge comes in. This book equips you with the tools to navigate the altcoin ecosystem confidently. From understanding blockchain technology and tokenomics to identifying red flags and evaluating real-world use cases, you'll gain the insights to make informed, strategic investments.

## What You'll Learn In This Book

Altcoin Edge is not just a primer—it's a roadmap to success in the altcoin market. Each chapter is a step forward in your journey, diving deep into the mechanics, opportunities, and risks of altcoin investments.

You'll learn about the different types of altcoins, from payment and utility tokens to governance and privacy coins. We'll explore how altcoins reshape industries, from decentralized finance to gaming and the metaverse. You'll discover how to evaluate altcoins critically, avoid scams, and identify projects with real potential. You'll also gain a clear understanding of the regulatory landscape, ensuring that you navigate this space responsibly.

This book contains real-world case studies, actionable insights, and strategies to help you build a diversified altcoin portfolio. Whether you're a seasoned crypto enthusiast or a newcomer eager to learn, Altcoin Edge offers something for everyone.

## Your Edge In The Altcoin Market

The altcoin market is a thrilling frontier, brimming

with innovation and opportunity. But with great potential comes great complexity. The market moves fast, trends shift quickly, and risks are ever-present. It would help if you had more than enthusiasm to thrive—knowledge, strategy, and a clear vision.

This book is your edge. It's your chance to confidently step into the world of altcoins, equipped with the insights and tools to identify the next big opportunities. It's your guide to navigating this dynamic landscape, spotting trends before they explode, and making investments that matter.

The altcoin revolution is here, and the future belongs to those who seize the moment. The next generation of crypto millionaires won't come from simply holding Bitcoin or Ethereum—they'll come from those who dared to explore the unknown and ventured into the diverse and exciting world of altcoins. So, are you ready to capture the growth beyond Bitcoin and Ethereum? Let's dive in. The altcoin edge awaits.

## How This Book Is Structured

To navigate the dynamic and often overwhelming world of altcoins, Altcoin Edge: Capturing Growth Beyond Bitcoin and Ethereum is organized into a clear, actionable framework. Each chapter builds upon the last, offering a comprehensive guide to understanding, evaluating, and capitalizing on altcoins' potential. Whether you're a seasoned crypto enthusiast or a newcomer eager to break into the market, this book is designed to provide valuable insights at every step of your journey.

## The Journey Through Altcoins

The book is divided into 15 chapters, each focusing on a specific aspect of the altcoin ecosystem. Here's a preview of how the book unfolds:

**Chapter 1:** The Foundations of Altcoins: Learn what altcoins are, why they exist, and how they differ from Bitcoin and Ethereum. This chapter sets the stage by highlighting their transformative potential.

**Chapter 2:** Blockchain Technology: Dive into the technology that powers altcoins. From consensus mechanisms to scalability and security, this chapter explains the nuts and bolts of blockchain innovation.

**Chapter 3:** DeFi Altcoins: Explore how altcoins are revolutionizing finance by creating decentralized platforms for lending, borrowing, and earning yields without traditional intermediaries.

**Chapter 4:** Gaming and Metaverse Altcoins: Discover how altcoins fuel virtual economies, from play-to-earn gaming models to metaverse platforms reshaping digital interaction.

**Chapter 5:** Privacy Coins: Understand privacy-focused altcoins' critical role in ensuring anonymity and security in an increasingly surveilled world.

**Chapter 6:** Green and Sustainable Altcoins: Examine how environmentally-conscious altcoins address cryptocurrencies' energy challenges, offering sustainable solutions for the future.

**Chapter 7:** Institutional Adoption: Learn how corporations and financial institutions leverage altcoins for enterprise solutions and what this means for market growth.

**Chapter 8:** Evaluating Altcoins: Gain insights into key metrics, tokenomics, and strategies to separate promising projects from scams.

**Chapter 9:** Risks and Challenges: Explore the risks associated with altcoin investments, from market volatility to regulatory hurdles, and how to navigate them successfully.

**Chapter 10:** Diversifying Your Portfolio: Learn strategies to build a balanced portfolio that minimizes risk while maximizing potential rewards in the altcoin market.

**Chapter 11:** The Community Ecosystem: Understand the importance of developer activity and community engagement in the success of an altcoin project.

**Chapter 12:** Regulation and Compliance: Navigate cryptocurrencies' evolving legal landscape and how they impact altcoin investments.

**Chapter 13:** Emerging Trends: Identify significant opportunities in cryptocurrency by analyzing emerging use cases and market dynamics.

**Chapter 14:** Case Studies of Success: This chapter provides detailed examples of altcoins that have disrupted industries and demonstrated what made them thrive.

**Chapter 15:** Your Altcoin Playbook: This comprehensive guide will help you craft your altcoin investment strategy and stay ahead in this fast-moving space.

## A Roadmap For All Levels

This book is structured to cater to readers with varying levels of crypto experience. The early chapters will build your foundational knowledge if you're new to cryptocurrencies. If you're familiar with Bitcoin and Ethereum, you'll appreciate the deep dives into altcoin-specific innovations and strategies. The content flows logically, allowing you to read from cover to cover or skip to specific chapters based on your interests. Each chapter includes practical takeaways, ensuring you can immediately apply your knowledge to your investment strategy.

## Why This Structure Works

The altcoin market is vast, fast-paced, and often intimidating. By breaking the book into focused, accessible chapters and sections, you'll understand this complex landscape clearly. Combining foundational concepts, real-world examples, and actionable strategies ensures you're equipped to learn about altcoins and thrive as an investor or enthusiast. Altcoin Edge is more than just a guide—it's your roadmap to capturing the next significant opportunities in cryptocurrency. Let the journey begin!

# PROLOGUE

*The Doge Millionaire: An Iconic Tale of Altcoin Success*

The cryptocurrency market is a fertile ground for stories that inspire, challenge conventions, and showcase the transformative power of innovation. Among these, Glauber Contessoto's ascent as the 'Doge Millionaire' shines as a beacon of the strength of the altcoin space. It's not just a narrative of wealth but a testament to the opportunities that abound in the cryptocurrency world. Dogecoin, the cryptocurrency at the heart of this tale, and Glauber's journey are perfect illustrations of how belief and innovation can defy expectations, empower individuals, and bring about life-altering outcomes.

The strength of the altcoin space lies in its diversity and potential for growth. Unlike Bitcoin and Ethereum, which dominate the market with their specific use cases and established infrastructures, altcoins like Dogecoin exist where experimentation, community-driven growth, and grassroots momentum thrive. Glauber's story demonstrates how individuals who recognize these opportunities and act decisively can achieve financial success. It's a testament to how unconventional thinking, belief in a project's potential, and the willingness to take calculated risks can pay off in the altcoin ecosystem.

Dogecoin is a unique player in the cryptocurrency world. It was created in 2013 as a parody of Bitcoin and inspired by the viral Doge meme featuring a Shiba Inu. While its origins were rooted in humor, the coin gradually developed a loyal community celebrating its accessibility and playful spirit. Unlike many cryptocurrencies that marketed themselves with complex technologies and lofty promises, Dogecoin embraced its lighthearted nature. This approach resonated with users who were often put off by traditional cryptocurrency projects' technical jargon and exclusivity.

The appeal of Dogecoin also lies in its simplicity and inclusivity. It wasn't trying to revolutionize finance or disrupt industries; it was just a fun, approachable digital currency that anyone could use or understand. This accessibility gave Dogecoin a unique edge, drawing in users curious about cryptocurrency but hesitant to dive into the more complex ecosystems of Bitcoin or Ethereum. The community became Dogecoin's most significant asset as enthusiastic users rallied around the coin, spreading awareness and creating a culture of support.

Glauber Contessoto recognized the potential of this community-driven momentum. In early 2021, as Dogecoin's popularity surged with the support of high-profile figures like Elon Musk, Glauber decided to make a bold move. At the time, Dogecoin was trading for fractions of a cent, largely dismissed by mainstream financial experts as a joke or speculative bubble. Glauber, however, saw something others did not: the coin's ability to capture the public imagination, driven by its growing online presence and a newfound surge of retail investor enthusiasm.

Glauber's decision to invest everything he had into Dogecoin was audacious, yet it underscored the unique opportunities within the altcoin space. Unlike Bitcoin, whose price had already reached heights that made substantial gains unlikely for small investors, Dogecoin offered the potential for exponential growth. Glauber's understanding of the market and his willingness to take risks enabled him to seize an opportunity that others overlooked. By February 2021, he had committed $250,000—his life savings and borrowed funds—to Dogecoin, believing it could change his life.

As the price of Dogecoin skyrocketed, Glauber's investment became the stuff of legend. By mid-April 2021, Dogecoin had surged by over 6,000%, transforming Glauber into a millionaire virtually overnight. His rise was a financial milestone and a cultural moment, capturing the attention of media outlets, social networks, and cryptocurrency enthusiasts worldwide. Glauber's story resonated because it represented the underdog narrative that Dogecoin itself embodied. He and the coin proved that success in the altcoin space sometimes relies on something other than technical sophistication but often hinges on timing, community, and belief.

One of the most compelling aspects of Glauber's journey was his decision to hold onto his investment despite the volatile nature of the cryptocurrency market. While many investors would have cashed out after achieving significant gains, Glauber chose to stay committed to Dogecoin, believing that the coin's potential was far from realized. His steadfastness earned him admiration within the Dogecoin community, which rallied around the mantra 'HODL' (Hold On for Dear Life), encouraging investors to resist selling during market dips. This term, often used humorously, reflects the community's belief in the coin's long-term potential and their commitment to weathering market fluctuations.

Glauber's dedication to Dogecoin extended beyond financial interests. He actively participated in the Dogecoin community, sharing his story and inspiring others to believe in the coin's potential. His openness and authenticity made him a relatable figure, and his rise as the "Doge Millionaire" symbolized the democratizing power of cryptocurrency. Dogecoin wasn't just a speculative asset but a movement that brought together people from diverse backgrounds, united by a shared belief in the coin and its representation.

The role of community in Dogecoin's success cannot be overstated. Unlike traditional investments driven by institutional support or corporate strategies, Dogecoin's rise was fueled by its grassroots following. Online platforms like Reddit and Twitter became hubs for Dogecoin enthusiasts, who used humor, memes, and camaraderie to promote the coin and foster a sense of belonging. This community-driven approach exemplifies the unique dynamics of the altcoin space, where sentiment, shared values, and collective action often play a more significant role than technical fundamentals.

Glauber's story also underscores the strategic importance of timing in the altcoin market. His decision to invest in Dogecoin came at a crucial juncture when the coin was undervalued but gaining traction among retail investors. This timing, coupled with the influence of social media and high-profile endorsements, set the stage for Dogecoin's meteoric rise. Glauber's success is a testament to how recognizing emerging trends and acting decisively can lead to significant returns in the fast-paced world of altcoins.

However, Glauber's journey has its lessons. The volatility of Dogecoin's price became evident as the market corrected in the months following its peak. After reaching an all-time high of $0.74 in May 2021, the coin's value declined, and Glauber's portfolio took a significant hit. Despite this downturn, he remained optimistic, continuing to hold his Dogecoin and reiterating his belief in its long-term potential. For Glauber, the investment was about more than financial gains; it was about being part of a movement democratizing access to financial opportunities.

The story of the Doge Millionaire underscores the risks and rewards inherent in the altcoin space. Glauber's decision to go all-in on Dogecoin was undeniably risky, and his unwavering commitment to holding through volatility highlights the potential for great rewards and the challenges of navigating the cryptocurrency market. His journey serves as a reminder that while altcoins can offer life-changing opportunities, they also require careful consideration, research, and an understanding of the risks involved. These risks include market volatility, regulatory uncertainty, and potential investment loss.

Dogecoin and the Doge Millionaire exemplify the unique strengths of the altcoin space. They demonstrate how community-driven projects can defy expectations, create value, and empower individuals to achieve financial success. Glauber's story is a testament to the transformative power of belief, timing, and the willingness to take risks in a space that rewards innovation and unconventional thinking. For those willing to embrace the opportunities within the altcoin market, the possibilities are as limitless as the imagination and determination to succeed.

And so, with the stage set by Dogecoin's improbable rise and the Doge Millionaire's bold journey, we now turn to the foundational elements of the altcoin universe, exploring the types of altcoins that are reshaping the cryptocurrency landscape and the roles they play in this transformative space.

# CHAPTER 1: THE FOUNDATIONS OF ALTCOINS

*"If you don't believe it or don't get it, I don't have the time to try to convince you, sorry."* — *Satoshi Nakamoto.*

Satoshi Nakamoto, the enigmatic creator of Bitcoin, encapsulates the spirit of independence and self-reliance that underpins the cryptocurrency movement. This statement challenges investors and enthusiasts to take ownership of their understanding, emphasizing that conviction in cryptocurrency comes from personal research and insight rather than external persuasion. This perspective holds even greater significance in the dynamic and often unpredictable altcoin market.

Altcoins, like Bitcoin, are built on complex technologies and innovative concepts that require a foundational understanding to appreciate their potential fully. Investors relying on superficial opinions or hype are likelier to fall prey to speculation and volatility. Satoshi's words remind us that the responsibility to grasp the nuances of the market lies with the individual. Only by conducting thorough research and engaging deeply with the principles of blockchain technology can investors develop the conviction needed to navigate this space confidently.

Moreover, Satoshi's unapologetic tone highlights the revolutionary ethos of cryptocurrency: it is not designed to cater to skeptics or followers. Instead, it empowers those willing to embrace its disruptive potential and explore its intricacies. This philosophy extends to altcoins, which challenge traditional financial systems and push the boundaries of innovation. For those who take the time to understand their value and possibilities, altcoins represent not just an investment but a step toward reshaping the future of finance.

◆ ◆ ◆

The world of cryptocurrency has captivated the imagination of millions, with Bitcoin and Ethereum leading the charge as the pioneers and powerhouses of this digital revolution. However, a vast, dynamic, and innovative universe lies beyond these giants: altcoins. Short for 'alternative coins,' altcoins represent any cryptocurrency other than Bitcoin. They are not just competitors to Bitcoin and Ethereum but are often solutions to their limitations, expanding blockchain technology's use cases and applications in groundbreaking ways. To understand the significance of altcoins, it is crucial to explore what they are, how they differ from the dominant players, and their unique roles in the ever-evolving cryptocurrency market.

Altcoins first emerged in the years following Bitcoin's creation in 2009. Bitcoin introduced the concept of a decentralized digital currency, challenging traditional financial systems. However, Bitcoin's design prioritized simplicity, security, and scarcity, which left room for improvement and diversification. As blockchain technology matured, developers sought to address Bitcoin's limitations, such as slow transaction speeds, high energy consumption, and limited programmability. The result was the birth of altcoins—cryptocurrencies that aimed to push the boundaries of blockchain technology and cater to specific niches.

Defining altcoins involves more than just labeling them as "not Bitcoin." Altcoins are a diverse group of cryptocurrencies, each with distinct purposes and innovations. While Bitcoin is often seen as "digital gold," prized for its scarcity and role as a store of value, altcoins span a spectrum of functionalities. Some, like Litecoin and Dash, focus on improving the speed and cost-efficiency of digital transactions. Others, such as Solana and Avalanche, prioritize scalability and network performance to support complex applications. Still, others like Monero and Zcash emphasize privacy, catering to users who value anonymity in an increasingly surveilled digital landscape.

The categories of altcoins reflect their diversity. Payment-focused altcoins aim to provide efficient and low-cost transaction systems, addressing the slow processing times and high fees that plague Bitcoin. Utility coins serve specific functions within blockchain ecosystems, enabling users to access services or interact with decentralized applications (dApps). Governance tokens empower holders to participate in decision-making processes within decentralized networks, embodying the principles of transparency and community-driven control. These distinctions underline the adaptability of altcoins, showcasing how they can fulfill specialized roles that Bitcoin and Ethereum were not designed to address, thereby providing a comprehensive view of the cryptocurrency market.

To fully grasp the role of altcoins, it is essential to understand their key differences from Bitcoin and Ethereum. As the first cryptocurrency, Bitcoin laid the foundation for decentralized finance with its simple yet revolutionary premise: a peer-to-peer digital currency that operates without a central authority. Its fixed supply and focus on security have made it a store of value akin to gold. Still, these very attributes also limit its utility. Bitcoin's transaction speeds are slow, its scalability is constrained, and its energy-intensive proof-of-work consensus mechanism has drawn criticism for its environmental impact.

Ethereum, introduced in 2015, built upon Bitcoin's foundation but took blockchain technology in a new direction. By enabling smart contracts—self-executing programs that run on the blockchain—Ethereum unlocked the potential for decentralized applications. This innovation turned Ethereum into a platform rather than just a currency, revolutionizing industries from finance to gaming. However, Ethereum's popularity has also exposed its limitations. High gas fees and network congestion have made it less accessible for smaller transactions and new users, and its transition to a proof-of-stake model to address these issues is still a work in progress.

Altcoins play a crucial role in filling the gaps left by Bitcoin and Ethereum. While Bitcoin focuses on stability and Ethereum on programmability, altcoins explore niches that require specialized solutions. For instance, Cardano emphasizes research-driven development and scalability, using a layered architecture to enhance performance and flexibility. With its lightning-fast transaction speeds and low fees, Solana has positioned itself as a platform for decentralized finance and gaming applications requiring high throughput. Privacy coins like Monero and Zcash cater to users who prioritize anonymity, offering features that Bitcoin and Ethereum can only provide with additional layers of technology.

The market roles of altcoins are as diverse as the cryptocurrencies themselves. They act as innovation drivers, pushing the boundaries of what blockchain technology can achieve. Altcoins are not constrained by the reputations and user expectations tied to Bitcoin and Ethereum, allowing them to experiment with new consensus mechanisms, governance models, and tokenomics. This freedom has led to breakthroughs such as proof-of-stake, a consensus algorithm that reduces energy consumption while maintaining network security, and interoperability protocols that connect different blockchains, creating more cohesive ecosystems.

Altcoins also play a crucial role in enabling industries to adopt blockchain technology. Many altcoins are designed with specific use cases in mind, making them ideal for real-world applications. In decentralized finance or DeFi, altcoins have had a significant impact. Projects like Uniswap, a decentralized exchange, and Aave, a decentralized lending platform, have revolutionized lending, borrowing, and trading by creating platforms without intermediaries. Gaming and virtual economies are another area of rapid growth, with altcoins powering play-to-earn models and virtual asset ownership in metaverse environments.

For investors, altcoins offer opportunities that Bitcoin and Ethereum cannot match. While Bitcoin and Ethereum are seen as relatively stable and established assets within the volatile cryptocurrency market, altcoins often experience dramatic price swings, offering the potential for substantial gains. This high-risk, high-reward dynamic can be exhilarating for seasoned traders and newcomers looking to capitalize on emerging trends. However, investing in altcoins requires careful research and a deep understanding of the market, as the same volatility that enables significant returns also carries the risk of loss. This cautionary note is essential to ensure that investors are well-prepared and informed when considering these investments.

Altcoins are also reshaping how we think about governance and community participation. In traditional systems, decision-making power is concentrated among a few individuals or entities.

Altcoins, particularly those with governance tokens, democratize control by giving stakeholders a voice. This community-driven approach ensures that users' interests are represented and aligns with the decentralized ethos of blockchain technology. Uniswap, a leading decentralized exchange, exemplifies this model, allowing token holders to vote on protocol changes and resource allocation. This community empowerment is a significant step towards a more democratic and inclusive financial system.

In summary, altcoins are far more than alternatives to Bitcoin and Ethereum. They represent the cutting edge of blockchain innovation, addressing the limitations of their predecessors and unlocking new possibilities for technology, industry, and investment. Understanding what altcoins are, their categories and distinctions, and their roles in the cryptocurrency market is beneficial and essential for anyone navigating this exciting and dynamic space. As we delve deeper into the world of altcoins, it becomes clear that they are not merely a supporting cast in the story of cryptocurrency—they are the architects of its future.

## *The Building Blocks of Altcoin Success*

The rise of altcoins in the cryptocurrency ecosystem has been revolutionary. While Bitcoin and Ethereum laid the groundwork for decentralized finance and blockchain applications, altcoins have pushed the boundaries of innovation, addressing limitations and expanding possibilities in ways that the earlier cryptocurrencies could not. To understand why altcoins are reshaping industries and transforming blockchain technology, we must examine the essential elements that contribute to their success. The foundation of any successful altcoin lies in three key building blocks: decentralized frameworks, robust community, and ecosystem support, as well as the ability to achieve scalability while maintaining usability.

**Decentralized Frameworks**
At the core of every successful altcoin is a decentralized framework. Decentralization is the defining feature of blockchain technology, ensuring that no single entity controls the network. This principle underpins the trust and security that cryptocurrencies offer. In contrast to traditional systems, which rely on centralized authorities like banks or governments, decentralized frameworks empower individuals to transact and interact without intermediaries.

Altcoins leverage decentralization in unique ways, often innovating beyond the original blockchain models established by Bitcoin and Ethereum. For example, Polkadot introduces a multichain architecture that allows different blockchains to interoperate seamlessly. This innovation addresses a key challenge in cryptocurrency: the inability of isolated blockchains to communicate and share data. Polkadot's decentralized framework enables the creation of a more connected and efficient ecosystem where diverse blockchains can collaborate to enhance their collective utility.

Another example is Avalanche, which uses a novel consensus mechanism called Avalanche Consensus.

This mechanism ensures high throughput and low latency while maintaining decentralization. Unlike Bitcoin's energy-intensive proof-of-work system or Ethereum's evolving proof-of-stake model, Avalanche achieves consensus through a lightweight and scalable process that can support thousands of transactions per second. This decentralization ensures security and enables the network to handle large-scale applications without compromising performance.

Decentralized frameworks are also integral to the governance models of many altcoins. By distributing decision-making power among community members, these frameworks align the interests of all stakeholders. Governance tokens, such as those used in protocols like Uniswap and MakerDAO, empower users to propose and vote on changes to the network. This participatory approach fosters transparency and accountability, ensuring that the network evolves in ways that reflect the needs and priorities of its users.

Ultimately, decentralized frameworks provide the foundation for altcoin success by combining security, transparency, and flexibility. They enable altcoins to operate as trustless systems where users can transact and interact without relying on intermediaries or centralized control. This revolutionary principle is essential for building resilient networks that adapt to changing market demands.

**Community and Ecosystem Support**
While technology is a critical factor in the success of an altcoin, the strength of its community and ecosystem often determines its long-term viability.

Unlike traditional financial systems or corporations, where a central authority drives growth and decision-making, altcoins rely on decentralized communities to build, maintain, and expand their networks. A vibrant community can be the difference between an altcoin that thrives and one that fades into obscurity.

The importance of community is evident in the case of Ethereum, which has one of the most robust and active developer ecosystems in the cryptocurrency space. Ethereum's community has built countless decentralized applications (dApps), from decentralized finance platforms to gaming and NFT marketplaces. This ecosystem of developers, users, and investors has created a network effect where each new application adds value to the Ethereum network, attracting more participants and driving further innovation.

Similarly, Cardano has cultivated a community centered on its commitment to research-driven development. Cardano's approach prioritizes academic rigor and peer-reviewed research, ensuring its technology is built on a solid foundation. This focus has attracted a community of developers and researchers dedicated to advancing blockchain technology in scalability, sustainability, and governance. The Cardano ecosystem is also supported by initiatives like Project Catalyst, which provides funding for community-driven proposals that enhance the network.

Community support extends beyond developers to include users, investors, and advocates who believe in an altcoin's vision. These stakeholders play a crucial role in spreading awareness, fostering adoption, and driving demand for the altcoin. In the case of

Dogecoin, for example, its enthusiastic and playful community has kept the coin relevant, even though it lacks the technical sophistication of other altcoins. This demonstrates the power of the community to sustain an altcoin's market presence, even without groundbreaking technology.

Ecosystem support is equally important, encompassing the infrastructure and partnerships that enable an altcoin to thrive. Exchanges, wallets, and payment processors that integrate with an altcoin contribute to its accessibility and usability. Partnerships with established companies or organizations can also enhance an altcoin's credibility and utility. For instance, Chainlink's partnerships with major companies have positioned it as a leader in decentralized Oracle solutions, enabling smart contracts to interact with real-world data.

By fostering strong communities and building supportive ecosystems, altcoins can achieve the network effects necessary for sustained growth and adoption. This emphasis on community and ecosystem development highlights blockchain technology's collaborative and decentralized nature, where success is driven by collective effort rather than centralized control.

**Scalability and Usability**
Scalability and usability are two crucial factors that determine the success of any altcoin in the cryptocurrency space. Scalability, the blockchain's ability to handle a growing number of transactions and users without delays or high fees, and usability, making blockchain technology accessible and intuitive, are key

to the evolution of altcoins.

Bitcoin and Ethereum, despite their pioneering roles, have faced scalability issues as their networks have grown. Bitcoin's limited block size and Ethereum's reliance on proof-of-work have resulted in slow transaction speeds and high fees during periods of high demand. These limitations have created opportunities for altcoins to innovate and address these challenges.

Solana is a prime example of an altcoin designed with scalability in mind. Thanks to its proof-of-history consensus mechanism, its high-performance blockchain can process tens of thousands of transactions per second. This innovation enables Solana to support decentralized finance applications, gaming platforms, and other high-throughput use cases without experiencing network congestion or exorbitant fees. Solana has positioned itself as a viable alternative to Ethereum for developers seeking fast and cost-effective solutions by prioritizing scalability.

Another example is Algorand, which combines scalability with security and decentralization through its pure proof-of-stake consensus mechanism. Algorand's design ensures the network can handle many transactions while maintaining low fees and minimal environmental impact. This scalability makes Algorand suitable for supply chain management, digital identity, and cross-border payments.

Usability is as important as scalability, as it determines how easily users and developers interact with an altcoin's network. Altcoins prioritizing user-friendly interfaces, seamless integration with wallets, and developer tools are more likely to be adopted. For example, Avalanche's platform offers customizable subnets, allowing developers to create blockchain networks tailored to their needs. This flexibility attracts various use cases, from financial services to gaming.

By achieving scalability and usability, altcoins can overcome the limitations of earlier blockchain networks and unlock new possibilities for adoption and growth. These attributes ensure that altcoins are not only technologically advanced but also accessible to a broader audience, making them indispensable in the evolution of blockchain technology.

The pillars of the cryptocurrency market's future are the building blocks of altcoin success—decentralized frameworks, community and ecosystem support, and scalability and usability. Decentralized frameworks ensure trust and security, empowering users to transact without intermediaries. Strong communities and ecosystems drive innovation, adoption, and network effects, creating the momentum necessary for sustained growth. Scalability and usability address the practical challenges of blockchain technology, making it more accessible and efficient.

As altcoins continue to push the boundaries of what is possible, these foundational elements will remain at the heart of their success. By understanding and leveraging these building blocks, altcoins can fulfill their potential to transform industries, redefine digital interactions, and shape the future of decentralized finance and technology. This potential is not just theoretical, but a real possibility that can inspire and give hope to those interested in the future of finance and technology.

## Types Of Altcoins To Know

Altcoins, the broader category of cryptocurrencies outside Bitcoin, represent a dynamic and diverse landscape. While Bitcoin laid the foundation for digital currencies, altcoins have evolved to fulfill specific roles, solve unique challenges, and expand the utility of blockchain technology. Among the many altcoins available, three categories stand out for their foundational importance and wide-ranging applications: payment coins, utility coins, and governance coins. Each type serves a distinct purpose, and understanding their characteristics is essential for grasping the broader implications of cryptocurrency innovation. This understanding will make you feel more informed and knowledgeable about the cryptocurrency landscape.

### Payment Coins: Redefining Transactions

Payment coins are the closest relatives to Bitcoin regarding their intended purpose. These cryptocurrencies are designed to facilitate transactions, acting as digital currencies that replace or supplement traditional money. Unlike Bitcoin, which has transitioned into a store of value and is often compared to digital gold, payment coins emphasize speed, efficiency, and affordability. They aim to overcome the limitations of fiat currencies and provide a seamless method for transferring value across borders without intermediaries like banks.

The primary appeal of payment coins lies in their ability

to process transactions quickly and cost-effectively. While traditional payment systems often incur high fees and require several days to settle international transfers, payment coins can execute transactions in seconds or minutes, often at a fraction of the cost. This speed and efficiency make them particularly attractive for microtransactions, remittances, and peer-to-peer transfers. For individuals in regions with limited access to banking infrastructure, payment coins offer a lifeline, enabling financial inclusion in ways traditional systems cannot.

Payment coins, beyond their transactional role, are pushing the boundaries of innovation. Many are incorporating advanced features like privacy and anonymity, enhancing user security and addressing concerns about surveillance and identity theft in the digital age.

Despite their benefits, payment coins are not without challenges. Scalability, especially for widely adopted coins, can lead to network congestion and slower transactions during peak demand. Regulatory scrutiny, particularly for privacy coins, can also create uncertainty. However, these challenges are being addressed by new projects that are leveraging innovative technologies and governance models.

**Utility Coins: Powering Blockchain Ecosystems**
Utility coins are a cornerstone of the cryptocurrency space, serving as the lifeblood of blockchain ecosystems. Unlike payment coins, which are primarily used for transactions, utility coins are designed to perform specific functions within their respective networks. They grant users access to services,

applications, and features integral to decentralized platforms' operation. By facilitating interactions within blockchain ecosystems, utility coins drive the adoption and development of blockchain technology across various industries.

One of the defining characteristics of utility coins is their ability to incentivize user participation. Blockchain networks often rely on decentralized, user-driven architectures, where participants contribute to the system's functionality and security. Utility coins reward users for their contributions, creating a self-sustaining ecosystem that benefits all participants. This incentive structure is particularly evident in decentralized storage networks, where users earn tokens to provide storage space or retrieve data.

Utility coins also play a critical role in enabling smart contracts and decentralized applications (dApps). These coins often serve as the currency for executing operations on the blockchain, such as deploying smart contracts, paying transaction fees, or accessing premium features within apps. For developers, utility coins provide a means of monetizing their applications, ensuring the ecosystem remains viable and scalable.

Beyond their technical functions, utility coins drive innovation in industries as diverse as finance, supply chain management, gaming, and healthcare. Utility coins underpin decentralized finance (DeFi) platforms in the financial sector, enabling users to lend, borrow, and trade assets without intermediaries. In supply chain management, these coins facilitate transparency and traceability, allowing stakeholders to verify the provenance of goods and ensure ethical practices.

In gaming, utility coins power virtual economies, enabling players to buy, sell, and trade in-game assets securely and transparently.

Despite their versatility, utility coins face several challenges. The success of a utility coin is closely tied to the adoption and growth of its underlying platform. Projects that need to gain traction or deliver on their promises often see their utility coins lose value, leaving investors and users disadvantaged. Moreover, the technical complexity of some platforms can deter mainstream adoption, particularly among non-technical users. To address these challenges, many blockchain projects prioritize user-friendly interfaces and robust developer tools to drive adoption and engagement.

**Governance Coins: Empowering Decentralized Decision-Making**
Governance coins represent a unique and transformative aspect of the cryptocurrency space. These coins are integral to decentralized networks, allowing stakeholders to participate in the decision-making processes that shape the platform's future. In traditional systems, decision-making authority is often centralized and concentrated in the hands of a few individuals or entities. Governance coins disrupt this model by democratizing control, giving users a direct voice in how a project evolves.

The rise of governance coins is rooted in the principles of decentralization and community ownership. By distributing governance power among token holders, these coins ensure that decisions align with the broader community's interests rather than a centralized authority. Governance coins are typically associated with decentralized autonomous organizations (DAOs) or platforms prioritizing community-driven development. Token holders can propose and vote on changes to the network, including updates to the protocol, allocation of resources, and integration of new features.

The power of governance coins lies in their ability to foster transparency and accountability. By making decision-making processes open and participatory, these coins reduce the risk of corruption and mismanagement. They also encourage collaboration and innovation as diverse stakeholders contribute their expertise and perspectives to decision-making. This approach aligns with the decentralized ethos of blockchain technology, where trust is distributed rather than concentrated.

Governance coins also serve as a tool for aligning incentives within a network. Token holders have a vested interest in the platform's success, as their tokens often increase in value when the network thrives. This creates a feedback loop where stakeholders are motivated to make decisions that benefit the long-term health of the ecosystem. These coins create a system that balances self-interest with collective benefit by tying governance power to economic incentives.

Despite their potential, governance coins face several challenges. One of the most significant is voter apathy, where token holders fail to participate in governance processes. Low voter turnout can lead to decisions that do not reflect the majority's interests, undermining the democratic principles of the system.

Additionally, governance coins can be vulnerable to centralization if a small number of entities accumulate a disproportionate amount of tokens, allowing them to exert outsized influence over the network.

To address these challenges, many platforms explore innovative governance models that encourage participation and prevent centralization. Some projects use delegation systems, where token holders can delegate voting power to trusted representatives. Others implement quadratic voting or other mechanisms that limit large stakeholders' influence while amplifying smaller participants' voices. These approaches aim to create a more equitable and inclusive governance system that reflects the values of decentralization.

The diversity of altcoins reflects the boundless potential of blockchain technology. Payment coins are revolutionizing how value is transferred, utility coins are powering the next generation of decentralized applications, and governance coins are reshaping how decisions are made in digital ecosystems. Each type of altcoin brings unique strengths and challenges, highlighting the versatility and innovation of the cryptocurrency space.

As blockchain technology evolves, these altcoins will play an increasingly important role in shaping the future of finance, technology, and governance. By understanding the characteristics and applications of payment, utility, and governance coins, we gain insight into the transformative power of cryptocurrencies and the opportunities they offer. In this dynamic and rapidly changing landscape, altcoins are not just alternatives but the architects of a decentralized future.

# CHAPTER 2: THE POWER OF BLOCKCHAIN TECHNOLOGY

*"The potential of blockchain technology goes far beyond just financial applications." — Vitalik Buterin.*

Vitalik Buterin, co-founder of Ethereum, illuminates the expansive capabilities of blockchain technology, highlighting that its impact transcends cryptocurrencies and financial transactions. While Bitcoin introduced the world to decentralized digital currency, blockchain's real power lies in its versatility and potential to revolutionize various industries. In supply chain management, blockchain enhances transparency by creating immutable records that track goods from origin to destination, ensuring authenticity and reducing fraud. Similarly, it secures patient data in healthcare, allowing for seamless yet private information sharing among authorized professionals.

Blockchain also paves the way for decentralized applications (dApps) and smart contracts—self-executing agreements that automate processes without requiring intermediaries, reducing costs and streamlining operations. Beyond these areas, blockchain holds promise in real estate, enabling tokenized ownership and simplifying property transactions, and in governance, where it can secure voting systems and improve transparency in public decision-making. By decoupling blockchain from its early association with cryptocurrency alone, Buterin emphasizes its role as a foundational technology with the power to transform industries, improve efficiency, and increase trust.

Buterin's perspective encourages us to view blockchain as more than a tool for financial innovation. It is a technology capable of reshaping society's operations, fostering new opportunities for collaboration, security, and progress across sectors far beyond finance. Blockchain is not just the technology of the future—it is already building a more efficient, transparent, and inclusive world today.

Blockchain technology, a transformative force of the 21st century, extends its disruptive potential beyond cryptocurrencies. While it's commonly associated with

Bitcoin and digital currencies, its reach spans across industries, promising to redefine how we store, share, and verify data. Understanding blockchain's core principles, mechanisms, and security features is not just essential, but it's also inspiring, as it unveils the power and potential of this innovative technology. This chapter delves into the foundational concepts of blockchain technology, explaining how it works, the consensus mechanisms that enable trust in decentralized systems, and the robust security features that make it one of the most secure forms of data management.

At its core, blockchain technology is a distributed ledger that records transactions across multiple computers to ensure transparency, security, and immutability. The term "blockchain" comes from its structure—a series of "blocks" of data linked together in a "chain." Each block contains a set of transactions, a timestamp, and a cryptographic hash of the previous block. This ensures that the chain cannot be altered retroactively without changing all subsequent blocks and gaining consensus from the network. This decentralized structure eliminates the need for a central authority, relying instead on the collective agreement of participants to validate and maintain the ledger's integrity.

The functionality of blockchain is built on a few key principles: decentralization, transparency, and immutability. The transparency of blockchain, which allows all network participants to view and verify transactions, fosters a sense of trust and confidence without the need for intermediaries. This, along with its decentralization and immutability, ensures the blockchain is resilient to failures or attacks on any individual node. Immutability, achieved through cryptographic hashing and consensus mechanisms, ensures that once a transaction is recorded on the blockchain, it cannot be altered or deleted, providing a reliable and tamper-proof record.

Understanding how blockchain works requires delving into the processes that enable its functionality. When a transaction is initiated, it is broadcast to the network, where nodes independently validate it based on predefined rules. Once validated, the transaction is grouped with others to form a block. This block is then added to the chain, with a cryptographic hash linking it to the previous block. The hash is a digital fingerprint unique to the block's content. Even the slightest change in the block's data would alter its hash, making tampering immediately evident. This cryptographic linkage between blocks ensures the integrity of the entire chain.

Consensus mechanisms are at the heart of blockchain's ability to operate without a central authority. They enable network participants to agree on the validity of transactions and maintain a consistent and unified ledger. Different blockchains employ various consensus mechanisms, each with its strengths and trade-offs. Proof of Work (PoW), for example, is the consensus mechanism used by Bitcoin. It requires nodes, known as miners, to solve complex mathematical puzzles to validate transactions and create new blocks. This process, while energy-intensive, ensures a high level of security by making it prohibitively expensive for any single entity to manipulate the blockchain.

Another widely used consensus mechanism is Proof of Stake (PoS), which relies on validators who stake their cryptocurrency as collateral to validate transactions. Unlike PoW, which requires computational power, PoS selects validators based on their stake size and participation history. This approach is more energy-efficient and scalable, making it a popular choice for newer blockchains. Delegated Proof of Stake (DPoS), a variation of PoS, introduces a system of voting where token holders elect delegates to validate transactions and make decisions on behalf of the network. This democratic approach combines efficiency with decentralization, fostering community involvement.

Other consensus mechanisms, such as Practical Byzantine Fault Tolerance (PBFT) and Proof of Authority (PoA), cater to specific use cases. PBFT is commonly used in private blockchains where participants are known and trusted, offering fast and reliable consensus. PoA, on the other hand, relies on a small number of pre-approved validators, making it suitable for applications where speed and simplicity are prioritized over decentralization. These diverse mechanisms highlight the adaptability of blockchain technology, which can be tailored to meet the needs of different networks and industries.

Security is one of the most compelling features of blockchain technology. Its decentralized nature ensures that there is no single point of failure, making it inherently resistant to hacking or tampering. To compromise a blockchain, an attacker would need to control a majority of the network's nodes, a feat that becomes increasingly difficult as the network grows.

This security is further bolstered by cryptographic techniques, which protect data from unauthorized access and ensure the authenticity of transactions.

Cryptographic hashing is a cornerstone of blockchain security. Hash functions take input data of any size and produce a fixed-length output, known as a hash. These functions are deterministic, meaning the same input will always produce the same hash, but even a minor change to the input will generate a completely different hash. This sensitivity to change makes hashing an effective tool for detecting tampering. In a blockchain, each block contains the previous block's hash, creating a chain of interdependent blocks. Any attempt to alter a block's data would invalidate its hash, breaking the chain and alerting the network to the tampering.

Digital signatures add another layer of security by ensuring the authenticity and integrity of transactions. When a user initiates a transaction, they sign it with their private key, creating a digital signature unique to that transaction. The recipient can verify the signature using the user's public key, confirming that the transaction originated from the sender and has not been altered. This cryptographic process ensures that transactions are secure and verifiable, even in a decentralized environment.

Blockchain networks also employ advanced cryptographic algorithms to protect sensitive data. While public blockchains prioritize transparency, private and permissioned blockchains often incorporate encryption to safeguard confidential information. Zero-knowledge proofs (ZKPs) are a notable innovation in this area. ZKPs allow one party to prove to another that a statement is true without revealing any underlying information. This technique is particularly valuable in applications such as identity verification and financial transactions, where privacy is paramount.

Another critical aspect of blockchain security is its resistance to double-spending, a problem that plagued early digital currencies. Double-spending occurs when the same digital asset is spent more than once. Blockchain solves this issue through its consensus mechanisms, which ensure that transactions are recorded chronologically and irreversibly. Once a transaction is included in a block and added to the chain, it becomes part of the permanent ledger, making double-spending impossible without gaining control of the network.

The immutability of blockchain records is a security feature and a foundation for trust. In traditional systems, data is often stored on centralized servers, vulnerable to manipulation, unauthorized access, and loss due to technical failures or malicious attacks. Blockchain's decentralized structure eliminates these vulnerabilities, providing a reliable and tamper-proof record. This attribute is particularly valuable in supply chain management, healthcare, and finance industries, where data integrity is critical.

Despite its strengths, blockchain security has challenges. The 51% attack, where an entity gains majority control of a network's nodes, remains a theoretical risk. Such an attack could allow the perpetrator to manipulate the blockchain, reversing transactions or creating fraud. However, the cost and complexity of executing a 51% attack increase exponentially with the size of the network, making it impractical for most blockchains.

The security of the blockchain also depends on the robustness of its smart contracts, which are self-executing programs that automate processes on the blockchain. Vulnerabilities in smart contracts can be exploited by attackers, leading to significant financial losses. To address this, developers employ rigorous testing and formal verification methods to ensure the reliability and security of smart contracts.

Blockchain technology's combination of decentralization, transparency, and robust security features makes it a powerful tool for addressing modern data management, finance, and beyond challenges. By eliminating intermediaries and creating trustless systems, blockchain empowers individuals and organizations to operate with greater efficiency, security, and autonomy. As the technology continues to evolve, its potential to reshape industries and redefine the digital landscape remains boundless. Understanding these foundational concepts is the first step in unlocking the transformative power of blockchain.

### Innovative Blockchain Applications

With its foundation of decentralization, transparency, and security, blockchain technology has unlocked a world of possibilities far beyond its origins in cryptocurrency. Developers and visionaries have explored new ways to leverage blockchain's capabilities as the technology has evolved, leading to a wave of innovative applications. Among the most transformative are Decentralized Finance (DeFi), Non-Fungible Tokens (NFTs), and Cross-Chain Interoperability. These applications are reshaping industries, creating new economic models, and driving the next phase of blockchain adoption.

**Decentralized Finance (DeFi): Redefining the Financial System**

Decentralized Finance, or DeFi, represents a paradigm shift in how financial services are conceived and delivered. Built on blockchain networks, DeFi eliminates the need for traditional intermediaries like banks, brokers, and clearinghouses. Instead, it relies on smart contracts—self-executing programs that automate financial transactions according to predefined rules. DeFi offers a decentralized alternative to traditional financial systems, directly providing services such as lending, borrowing, trading, and investing to users.

The appeal of DeFi lies in its accessibility and inclusivity. Traditional financial systems often exclude individuals who need access to banks or credit, especially in developing regions. DeFi platforms, however, are open to anyone with an internet connection and a digital wallet, making financial services more accessible. This inclusivity has contributed to the rapid growth of DeFi, with billions of dollars in assets locked into decentralized protocols across various blockchain networks.

DeFi also empowers users by giving them greater control over their financial assets. In traditional systems, individuals must trust intermediaries to manage their funds, often at the cost of high fees and limited transparency. DeFi eliminates these intermediaries, enabling users to transact and invest directly. For instance, individuals can lend their cryptocurrency to a DeFi protocol and earn interest without relying on a bank. Similarly, they can trade digital assets on decentralized exchanges (DEXs) without surrendering custody of their funds.

The flexibility of DeFi has led to the creation of innovative financial instruments and services. Yield farming, for example, allows users to maximize returns by moving their assets across different protocols to take advantage of varying interest rates. Stablecoins, a subset of cryptocurrencies pegged to stable assets like fiat currencies, provide a reliable medium of exchange within DeFi ecosystems. These innovations are not only attracting retail investors but also drawing the attention of institutional players, further legitimizing the DeFi space.

Despite its promise, DeFi has challenges. The reliance on smart contracts, while enabling automation, also introduces vulnerabilities. Bugs or coding errors in smart contracts can be exploited, leading to significant financial losses. Furthermore, the lack of regulatory oversight raises concerns about consumer protection, fraud, and systemic risks. These challenges highlight the need for greater transparency, robust security measures, and collaborative efforts between developers and regulators to ensure the sustainable growth of DeFi.

**Non-Fungible Tokens (NFTs): Redefining Ownership and Creativity**
Non-fungible tokens, or NFTs, have emerged as one of the most talked-about applications of blockchain

technology. Unlike cryptocurrencies such as Bitcoin or Ethereum, which are fungible and interchangeable, NFTs represent unique digital assets that cannot be replicated or replaced. This uniqueness is encoded on the blockchain, creating a verifiable record of ownership and authenticity. NFTs have revolutionized the concept of ownership, particularly in the realms of art, music, gaming, and collectibles.

The rise of NFTs has created a new economy for digital creators. Before blockchain technology, digital art and content were easily copied and shared, making it challenging for creators to monetize their work effectively. NFTs solve this problem by assigning ownership rights to digital assets, enabling creators to sell their work directly to buyers while retaining a share of future sales through royalties. This has empowered artists, musicians, and creators to connect with their audiences in new and meaningful ways.

In the art world, NFTs have disrupted traditional systems of curation and distribution. Artists can now mint their work as NFTs and sell them on decentralized marketplaces, bypassing galleries and auction houses. This democratization of the art market has allowed emerging artists to gain recognition and monetize their work without intermediaries. High-profile sales, such as Beeple's digital artwork "Everydays: The First 5000 Days," which sold for $69 million at a Christie's auction, have highlighted the immense potential of NFTs in transforming the art industry.

Beyond art, NFTs are driving innovation in gaming and virtual worlds. In blockchain-based games, NFTs represent in-game assets, such as characters, weapons, and land. Unlike traditional games, where assets are locked within the game's ecosystem, blockchain games allow players to own their assets fully. These assets can be traded, sold, or used across multiple games and platforms, creating a player-driven economy. The concept of the metaverse, a shared virtual space where users can interact and create, is also being shaped by NFTs, which provide the foundation for virtual ownership and identity.

NFTs are not without their controversies. The environmental impact of minting NFTs, which often rely on energy-intensive blockchain networks, has sparked criticism. Additionally, the speculative nature of the NFT market has led to concerns about bubbles and volatility, with some critics questioning the long-term value of digital assets. Despite these challenges, the underlying technology of NFTs holds immense potential, particularly as the industry explores more sustainable and accessible models.

## Cross-Chain Interoperability: Bridging the Blockchain Ecosystem

As blockchain technology has matured, blockchain networks have grown exponentially. While this diversity has fostered innovation, it has created a fragmented ecosystem where networks operate in isolation. Cross-chain interoperability addresses this challenge by enabling different blockchains to communicate and share data seamlessly. This capability is essential for unlocking the full potential of blockchain technology and fostering collaboration across networks.

Interoperability, a crucial aspect of blockchain

technology, plays a pivotal role in the context of decentralized finance. Many DeFi applications are confined to specific blockchain networks, limiting their accessibility and functionality. For instance, a user with assets on the Ethereum blockchain may wish to engage with a DeFi protocol on the Binance Smart Chain, a task made possible only through interoperability solutions. Cross-chain protocols bridge this gap, enabling users to transfer assets and data across networks, thereby creating a more connected and efficient ecosystem.

One of the key innovations driving cross-chain interoperability is the development of blockchain bridges. These bridges enable the transfer of assets and information between blockchains, often through the use of wrapped tokens. For instance, Bitcoin can be represented as Wrapped Bitcoin (WBTC) on the Ethereum blockchain, allowing Bitcoin holders to participate in Ethereum-based DeFi applications. This integration not only enhances the utility of individual blockchains but also creates synergies that drive the growth of the broader ecosystem.

Interoperability also plays a critical role in enhancing scalability. As blockchain networks grow, they often need more transaction speed and capacity. Interoperability solutions allow networks to share workloads, distribute transactions across multiple chains, and reduce congestion. This approach is particularly valuable in high-demand applications like DeFi and gaming, where scalability is crucial for user experience.

The potential of cross-chain interoperability extends beyond financial applications. In supply chain management, for example, interoperability allows different stakeholders to collaborate on shared platforms, thereby enhancing transparency and efficiency. In healthcare, it enables the secure sharing of patient data across institutions, fostering better coordination and outcomes. By breaking down silos, cross-chain interoperability is driving the adoption of blockchain technology across diverse industries, demonstrating its potential in non-financial applications.

Despite its promise, achieving interoperability is a complex technical challenge. Blockchains differ in architectures, consensus mechanisms, and protocols, making integration difficult. Security is another concern, as bridges and interoperability solutions can introduce vulnerabilities. To address these challenges, developers are exploring new technologies, such as parachains and layer-two solutions, that enhance compatibility and scalability while maintaining security. This ongoing effort to overcome these challenges underscores the industry's commitment to realizing the full potential of blockchain technology.

## The Transformative Potential of Blockchain Applications

The innovative applications of blockchain technology —DeFi, NFTs, and cross-chain interoperability—are reshaping industries and creating new possibilities for individuals, businesses, and communities. DeFi is revolutionizing financial systems by providing decentralized alternatives to traditional services. NFTs are redefining ownership and creativity, empowering creators, and transforming how digital assets are valued. Cross-chain interoperability is bridging the blockchain ecosystem, fostering collaboration, and unlocking the full potential of blockchain technology. These developments underscore the transformative power of blockchain technology and inspire optimism about the future of the digital age.

As these applications continue to evolve, they highlight blockchain's versatility and transformative power. They also underscore the importance of collaboration and innovation in overcoming challenges and driving adoption. By exploring these groundbreaking use cases, we gain a deeper understanding of how blockchain technology shapes the future and redefines what is possible in the digital age. This collaborative nature of blockchain technology makes us all part of a larger community, working together to push the boundaries of what is possible.

**Altcoins Leading Blockchain Innovation**
Blockchain technology has evolved rapidly since Bitcoin's inception, growing beyond its initial purpose as a decentralized currency system. Today, blockchain underpins an ecosystem of innovative solutions to address real-world challenges and expand decentralized networks' utility. Altcoins have emerged as the vanguard of this innovation, pushing the boundaries of scalability, interoperability, and decentralization. Among these, Polkadot, Avalanche, and Algorand stand out as leaders, each offering unique advancements that address critical limitations of earlier blockchain systems while laying the foundation for future developments.

**Polkadot: Connecting Blockchains**

The blockchain ecosystem has traditionally been fragmented, with networks operating in isolation and needing help communicating or collaborating effectively. Polkadot was created to address this challenge by enabling seamless interoperability among blockchains. Designed by Gavin Wood, one of the co-founders of Ethereum, Polkadot is a multichain framework that connects independent blockchains into a unified network, allowing them to share information and assets securely.

Polkadot's architecture is built around a central relay chain, which coordinates the network and maintains its security. Connected to the relay chain are para chains—individual blockchains optimized for specific use cases. Each para chain operates independently, with its own governance, tokens, and functionality, but it all benefits from the shared security and interoperability provided by the relay chain. This structure allows Polkadot to combine the strengths of independent blockchains while overcoming their isolation, creating a more cohesive and collaborative ecosystem.

One of Polkadot's most significant contributions to blockchain innovation is its ability to facilitate specialized blockchains. Traditional blockchains like Ethereum aim to be general-purpose platforms supporting various applications. While this approach offers flexibility, it often leads to inefficiencies and congestion, particularly during periods of high demand. Polkadot's parachain model allows developers to create blockchains tailored to specific needs, such as finance, supply chain management, or gaming, without competing for resources on a single network. This specialization enhances performance and scalability while enabling the development of highly efficient applications.

Polkadot also emphasizes governance and adaptability. Its on-chain governance system allows stakeholders to participate directly in decision-making processes, ensuring that the network evolves according to community needs. This model reduces reliance on hard forks, which can be divisive and disruptive, by enabling seamless upgrades and improvements through consensus. Polkadot's approach reflects a broader trend in blockchain toward decentralization in technology and governance, fostering transparency and collaboration.

**Avalanche: High-Performance Scaling**
Scalability has been one of the most persistent challenges in blockchain technology. While revolutionary, networks like Bitcoin and Ethereum have faced significant limitations in transaction throughput, leading to delays and high fees during periods of congestion. Avalanche was created to address these issues, offering a high-performance platform designed for speed, efficiency, and flexibility.

Avalanche's architecture is based on a novel consensus mechanism called Avalanche Consensus. Unlike traditional models such as Proof of Work (PoW) or Proof of Stake (PoS), Avalanche Consensus achieves consensus through repeated random sampling and lightweight voting. This process enables rapid finality, meaning that transactions are confirmed in seconds and cannot be reversed. The speed and efficiency of this consensus mechanism make Avalanche one of the fastest blockchains available, capable of processing thousands of transactions per second while maintaining low fees.

A key innovation of Avalanche is its support for subnetworks or subnets. These are customizable blockchain networks that operate within the Avalanche ecosystem. Subnets allow developers to create blockchains tailored to specific applications, with control over parameters such as consensus rules, governance, and tokenomics. For example, a financial institution might use a subnet to build a private blockchain for secure transactions, while a gaming company could create a public blockchain optimized for virtual economies. This flexibility enables Avalanche to support various use cases, from decentralized finance (DeFi) to enterprise applications.

Avalanche also prioritizes interoperability, both within its ecosystem and across external blockchains. The Avalanche Bridge, a cross-chain bridge, enables users to transfer assets between Avalanche and other networks like Ethereum. This interoperability enhances Avalanche's utility, allowing it to serve as a hub for decentralized applications and assets from multiple ecosystems. By connecting disparate networks, Avalanche fosters collaboration and synergy, driving the growth of the blockchain space.

In addition to its technical achievements, Avalanche emphasizes environmental sustainability. Its consensus mechanism is far more energy-efficient than PoW, aligning with growing concerns about blockchain technology's environmental impact. This focus on sustainability makes Avalanche an attractive platform for developers and organizations seeking to build environmentally responsible applications.

## Algorand: Bridging Decentralization and Speed

Algorand was designed to solve the blockchain trilemma—the challenge of achieving scalability, security, and decentralization simultaneously. Many blockchains sacrifice one of these attributes to optimize the other two, but Algorand aims to strike a balance by combining innovative technology with a robust consensus mechanism. Founded by MIT professor and Turing Award winner Silvio Micali, Algorand is built on a pure Proof of Stake (PPoS) consensus protocol, which enables high performance while maintaining decentralization.

PPoS differs from traditional PoS by selecting validators randomly and proportionally to their stake in the network. This process ensures fairness and prevents centralization, as every token holder can participate in consensus. The randomness of validator selection also enhances security by making it difficult for attackers to predict and target specific nodes. Algorand's consensus mechanism enables the network to process transactions quickly, with finality achieved in seconds, making it suitable for applications requiring high throughput and low latency.

One of Algorand's defining features is its focus on simplicity and accessibility. Unlike blockchains requiring complex development tools or specialized knowledge, Algorand offers a user-friendly platform that supports a wide range of programming languages and tools. This accessibility has attracted developers from diverse industries, fostering the creation of innovative applications in finance, healthcare, supply chain management, and beyond.

Algorand has made significant strides in promoting sustainability. Its consensus mechanism is inherently energy-efficient, as it does not require the extensive computational power PoW systems use. In 2021, Algorand became the first blockchain to achieve carbon neutrality, offsetting its small energy footprint through partnerships with environmental organizations. This commitment to sustainability aligns with the values of businesses and developers seeking to build impactful and responsible applications.

Interoperability is another area where Algorand excels. The network supports atomic swaps and cross-chain bridges, enabling seamless interaction with other blockchains. Algorand's compatibility with Ethereum and other platforms enhances its utility, allowing developers to build applications that leverage the strengths of multiple ecosystems. This interoperability positions Algorand as a key player in the emerging multichain future, where collaboration and integration drive the growth of the blockchain space.

**The Future of Blockchain Innovation**
Polkadot, Avalanche, and Algorand exemplify the diverse and innovative approaches altcoins are taking to address the challenges of blockchain technology. Polkadot's focus on interoperability and specialization enables collaboration and efficiency across independent blockchains. Avalanche's high-performance platform offers speed, flexibility, and sustainability, making it ideal for a wide range of applications. Algorand's balanced approach to decentralization, scalability, and

accessibility demonstrates the potential for blockchain to achieve the best of all worlds.

These altcoins are not merely alternatives to Bitcoin or Ethereum; they are leaders in a new wave of blockchain innovation, driving advancements that will shape the future of technology, finance, and governance. By addressing critical limitations and exploring new possibilities, Polkadot, Avalanche, and Algorand are paving the way for an interconnected, efficient, and sustainable decentralized future. As blockchain technology evolves, these projects will play a pivotal role in realizing its transformative potential.

# CHAPTER 3: DEFI ALTCOINS

*"Decentralized finance is redefining the financial landscape, making it more inclusive and transparent."* — Tyler Winklevoss

Winklevoss highlights the transformative power of decentralized finance (DeFi), reshaping the financial system by removing traditional gatekeepers and creating open, accessible markets. DeFi altcoins are at the heart of this movement, enabling services such as lending, borrowing, trading, and earning interest—all without intermediaries like banks or brokers. Using blockchain technology, DeFi creates transparent, secure, and available systems for anyone with an internet connection.

One of DeFi's greatest achievements is its inclusivity. Traditional financial systems often exclude individuals due to barriers such as geography, creditworthiness, or lack of access to banking infrastructure. DeFi eliminates these obstacles, offering financial tools to anyone, regardless of their location or socioeconomic status. This democratization of finance is a significant step toward closing the global financial inclusion gap. Transparency is another cornerstone of DeFi. All transactions are recorded on a public blockchain, ensuring accountability and reducing the risk of fraud. Users can verify the processes themselves, fostering trust that traditional systems struggle to achieve. DeFi altcoins empower individuals by giving them complete control over their assets and financial decisions.

Winklevoss's observation reflects DeFi's revolutionary nature. By decentralizing and democratizing finance, DeFi is not only disrupting traditional models but also laying the groundwork for a more equitable and transparent financial future. DeFi altcoins drive this change, offering new opportunities and challenging the status quo.

The rise of decentralized finance, or DeFi, marks a seismic shift in the financial landscape, offering a glimpse into a future where traditional intermediaries and centralized institutions no longer hold sway over economic activity. DeFi, powered by blockchain technology and altcoins, is crafting a financial ecosystem that is open, transparent, and borderless. It does away with the need for intermediaries, replacing them with decentralized protocols that offer a wide array of financial services. From lending and borrowing to trading and investing, DeFi altcoins are the driving force behind this revolution, fostering innovation and empowering individuals to shape their financial destinies.

To understand DeFi, it is essential to grasp its fundamental principles. At its core, DeFi seeks to democratize access to financial services by leveraging the transparency and immutability of blockchain technology. Traditional finance relies on centralized institutions like banks, credit unions, and governments to provide services and enforce rules. These institutions act as intermediaries, ensuring trust and security but often at the cost of efficiency, inclusivity, and transparency. DeFi, by contrast, operates on decentralized networks where smart contracts—self-executing programs encoded on a blockchain—automate and enforce financial transactions. This decentralization removes the need for intermediaries, placing power directly in the hands of users.

One of the foundational principles of DeFi is permissionlessness. In traditional finance, access to services often depends on geographic location, credit history, or financial status. This exclusivity can marginalize individuals and communities, particularly in developing regions. DeFi, however, is open to anyone with an internet connection and a digital wallet. There are no gatekeepers or prerequisites, making it a truly inclusive system. This openness expands access and fosters innovation as developers worldwide contribute to the growth of DeFi protocols and applications.

Transparency is not just a feature of DeFi, it's a cornerstone. Traditional financial systems often operate within opaque frameworks, where users have limited visibility into decisions or how funds are managed. In contrast, DeFi operates on public blockchains where all transactions, smart contracts, and protocol rules are visible to anyone. This transparency builds trust and accountability, as users can verify the integrity of the system for themselves. It also reduces the risk of corruption and fraud, prevalent in opaque, centralized systems. This transparency is a key advantage of DeFi, providing users with a level of trust and security that is often lacking in traditional finance.

Interoperability is a unique aspect of DeFi, allowing different protocols and platforms to interact seamlessly. This interconnectedness enables users to access a wide range of services from a single wallet or interface, creating a unified financial ecosystem. For example, a user might deposit funds into a DeFi lending protocol, use the earned interest to trade assets on a decentralized exchange, and reinvest profits into yield farming—all without leaving the DeFi ecosystem. This level of flexibility and integration is unprecedented in traditional finance.

The benefits of decentralization go beyond convenience. One of the most significant advantages is security. In centralized systems, a single point of failure —such as a compromised server or corrupt official— can lead to catastrophic losses. DeFi systems distribute risk across a network of nodes, making them far more resilient to attacks and failures. DeFi protocols also employ cryptographic security measures to protect user data and funds, ensuring participants retain control over their assets.

DeFi is not just about cutting out the middleman, it's about efficiency. Traditional financial systems often involve layers of intermediaries, each adding transaction costs and delays. DeFi streamlines these processes by replacing intermediaries with smart contracts, which execute transactions automatically and in real time. For example, a user can borrow funds from a DeFi protocol without needing a credit check or approval from a bank. The transaction is governed entirely by code, ensuring the terms are met, and the process is completed efficiently. This efficiency is a key advantage of DeFi, offering users a level of convenience and speed that is often lacking in traditional finance.

DeFi is not just about financial transactions, it's about empowerment. It gives users a sense of control and independence that is often lacking in traditional financial systems. In the traditional setup, users must entrust their funds to banks, brokers, or other intermediaries, which may charge high fees or impose restrictions. DeFi changes this dynamic, allowing users to retain full custody of their assets. This means they can transact, invest, and earn yields without relying on third parties. This self-sovereignty aligns with the broader ethos of blockchain technology, which prioritizes individual empowerment and decentralization.

While DeFi offers numerous advantages, it is important to understand how it differs from traditional finance. One of the most obvious distinctions is the absence of centralized intermediaries. Banks, brokers, and clearinghouses are trusted third parties in conventional systems that facilitate transactions, enforce contracts, and manage risks. These intermediaries provide stability but often at the cost of transparency, efficiency, and accessibility. DeFi eliminates these intermediaries, relying instead on decentralized protocols and smart contracts to perform the same functions.

The lack of intermediaries in DeFi leads to a fundamental shift in how trust is established. Trust is placed in institutions, regulators, and legal frameworks in traditional finance. DeFi replaces this institutional trust with "trustless" systems that operate autonomously based on code. Users do not need to trust a central authority; they only need to trust the underlying technology and the integrity of the network. This shift democratizes access to financial services, as users can participate without relying on centralized gatekeepers.

Another key difference is DeFi's level of transparency. Traditional financial systems are often opaque, with limited visibility into how funds are managed or how decisions are made. This opacity can lead to inefficiencies, corruption, and a lack of accountability. DeFi, on the other hand, operates on public blockchains where all transactions and smart contracts are visible and verifiable. This transparency builds trust among participants and reduces the likelihood of fraud or mismanagement.

Another major differentiator is DeFi's accessibility. Traditional finance is often exclusionary, with barriers such as credit requirements, geographic restrictions, and high fees limiting access to services. DeFi, by contrast, is open to anyone with a digital wallet, regardless of their background or financial status. This inclusivity is particularly valuable in developing regions, where many individuals lack access to traditional banking infrastructure. By removing these barriers, DeFi has the potential to foster financial inclusion on a global scale.

The speed and efficiency of DeFi also set it apart. Traditional financial transactions, especially those involving cross-border payments or complex instruments, can take days to settle and incur significant fees. DeFi transactions, however, are executed almost instantly and at a fraction of the cost. This efficiency is especially beneficial for users in developing countries, where remittance fees can consume a significant portion of transferred funds. DeFi protocols enable individuals to send and receive money quickly and affordably, empowering them to participate in the global economy.

Despite these advantages, DeFi has its challenges. While enabling automation and efficiency, the reliance on smart contracts also introduces risks. Bugs or vulnerabilities in smart contracts can be exploited by malicious actors, leading to significant financial losses. Additionally, the lack of regulatory oversight in DeFi raises concerns about consumer protection, fraud, and systemic risks. These challenges highlight the need for robust security measures, transparent governance, and collaboration between developers, regulators, and users to ensure the sustainable growth of DeFi.

Understanding decentralized finance requires more than a technical appreciation of blockchain technology. It necessitates recognition of decentralization's transformative potential and the ways it challenges the status quo. By removing intermediaries, enhancing transparency, and expanding accessibility, DeFi redefines what is possible in finance. Altcoins designed for DeFi are at the forefront of this revolution, offering new opportunities for innovation, empowerment, and economic growth.

DeFi altcoins are not merely financial tools but the building blocks of a decentralized future. They enable individuals to participate in a global financial system that is more inclusive, efficient, and transparent than anything that has come before. As we delve deeper into the applications and implications of DeFi, it becomes clear that this movement is not just about technology —it is about creating a more equitable and accessible financial system for everyone.

## Key Defi Projects

Decentralized finance, or DeFi, redefines the global financial landscape by offering a decentralized, transparent, and efficient alternative to traditional systems. At the heart of this revolution are DeFi projects that use blockchain technology and altcoins to provide financial services like trading, lending, and currency stability. These projects have become popular, enabling users to bypass intermediaries and engage directly with decentralized protocols. Uniswap, Aave, and MakerDAO are among the most impactful projects. Each has carved out a distinct niche in the DeFi ecosystem, pushing the boundaries of what decentralized finance can achieve.

Uniswap, one of the earliest and most influential

decentralized exchanges (DEXs), revolutionized how users trade cryptocurrencies. Traditional centralized and decentralized exchanges typically relied on order books to match buyers and sellers. While functional, this system could have been more efficient, especially for less popular tokens, as it required a consistent balance of demand and supply. Uniswap eliminated the need for order books by introducing an innovative automated market maker (AMM) model. In this model, users trade directly against liquidity pools, which are collections of tokens provided by other users. This approach ensures continuous liquidity for all listed tokens, regardless of popularity, and eliminates the delays associated with traditional trading methods.

The impact of Uniswap extends beyond its technological innovation. By removing barriers to entry, it democratized access to trading, allowing anyone with a digital wallet to swap tokens seamlessly. Uniswap'sUniswap's user-friendly interface and transparent fee structure further contributed to its widespread adoption. The platform's native token, UNI, added another layer of value by enabling holders to participate in governance decisions, such as fee adjustments and protocol upgrades. This decentralized governance model exemplifies the ethos of DeFi, where power and decision-making are distributed among users rather than concentrated in a central authority.

Uniswap's success inspired a wave of innovation in the DEX space, with numerous projects adopting and building upon its AMM model. This competition spurred advancements in liquidity provision, fee optimization, and user experience, driving the entire DeFi ecosystem forward. Uniswap's open-source nature further fueled this growth as developers worldwide contributed to its evolution and created complementary tools and services. The project's influence is evident in its billions of dollars in daily trading volume and its role as a catalyst for the broader adoption of DeFi.

While Uniswap redefined token trading, Aave transformed how users approach lending and borrowing in the DeFi space. Traditional lending systems are often plagued by inefficiencies, high fees, and restricted access, particularly for individuals without strong credit histories. Aave disrupted this model by creating a decentralized lending platform without intermediaries. Instead of relying on banks or credit unions, Aave connects borrowers and lenders directly through smart contracts, ensuring transparency, security, and efficiency.

One of Aave's most notable innovations is the introduction of flash loans, a groundbreaking concept that allows users to borrow assets without collateral, provided the loan is repaid within the same transaction. Flash loans enable complex financial operations, such as arbitrage and debt restructuring, that were previously inaccessible to most users. This innovation not only expanded the functionality of DeFi but also showcased the potential of smart contracts to automate and streamline financial processes.

Aave's flexibility extends to its support for a wide range of assets and unique approach to collateralization. Users can deposit a variety of cryptocurrencies as collateral and borrow against their holdings at competitive rates. The platform's interest rates are determined algorithmically based on supply and demand, ensuring a fair and dynamic pricing structure. This model incentivizes borrowing and lending, creating a self-sustaining ecosystem that benefits all participants.

The AAVE token is central to the platform's platform'splatform's governance and risk management. Token holders can vote on key protocol decisions, such as asset inclusion and risk parameters, ensuring that the platform evolves in line with the needs of its community. Aave's decentralized governance model reflects the broader trend in DeFi toward community-driven development, where users have a direct stake in the success of the projects they support.

Aave's impact on the DeFi space is profound, as it has made borrowing and lending more accessible, efficient, and transparent. Its success has inspired similar projects, each building on Aave's innovations to create more robust and user-friendly lending solutions. By breaking down barriers and empowering users, Aave has set a new standard for decentralized finance, demonstrating the transformative potential of blockchain technology.

While Uniswap and Aave address trading and lending, MakerDAO focuses on one of the most fundamental challenges in cryptocurrency: stability. Cryptocurrencies are notorious for their volatility, which can hinder their adoption as a medium of exchange or store of value. MakerDAO tackled this issue by creating DAI, a stablecoin pegged to the value of the US dollar. Unlike traditional stablecoins, backed by fiat reserves held by centralized entities, DAI is fully decentralized and collateralized by a diverse range of cryptocurrencies.

MakerDAO's innovative approach to stability relies on a system of smart contracts and collateralized debt positions (CDPs). Users can lock up their cryptocurrency assets as collateral in a smart contract to generate DAI, which can then be used for transactions, investments, or savings. The collateral-to-debt ratio is carefully managed to ensure the stability of DAI, with liquidation mechanisms in place to prevent under-collateralization. This system creates a stable and transparent currency that retains the benefits of decentralization while mitigating the risks of volatility.

The MKR token is vital in MakerDAO's governance and risk management. MKR holders can vote on key decisions like collateral types, stability fees, and risk parameters. This decentralized governance model ensures that MakerDAO remains adaptable and responsive to changing market conditions. MKR holders are also responsible for maintaining the system's stability, as they are the first to absorb losses in the event of a collateral shortfall. This alignment of incentives creates a robust and sustainable ecosystem that benefits all participants.

MakerDAO's influence extends beyond its role as a stablecoin provider. Creating a decentralized and transparent system for stability has set a new benchmark for financial innovation in the cryptocurrency space. DAI's widespread adoption across DeFi platforms and use cases demonstrates its utility and effectiveness as a stable and reliable currency. MakerDAO's success has also inspired the development of similar projects, further advancing the DeFi ecosystem and expanding the use cases for stablecoins.

The collective contributions of Uniswap, Aave, and MakerDAO highlight the transformative potential of DeFi altcoins. Each project addresses a specific need within the financial ecosystem, from trading and lending to stability, while demonstrating the power of decentralization, transparency, and community-driven development. These projects exemplify the innovation happening in the DeFi space and underscore the importance of user-centric design and governance in creating sustainable and impactful solutions.

The growth and success of these key DeFi projects have had a ripple effect across the cryptocurrency space, inspiring new entrants and driving the broader adoption of decentralized finance. By pushing the boundaries of what is possible with blockchain technology, Uniswap, Aave, and MakerDAO are shaping the future of finance and paving the way for a more inclusive, efficient, and decentralized financial system. As the DeFi ecosystem evolves, these projects will remain at the forefront of innovation, setting the standard for the next generation of financial services.

## The Future Of Defi Altcoins

Decentralized finance, or DeFi, has emerged as one of the most transformative sectors within the blockchain space. By leveraging decentralized protocols, smart contracts, and altcoins, DeFi has reimagined traditional financial services and introduced new paradigms of efficiency, accessibility, and inclusivity. The future of DeFi altcoins holds immense potential, with the continuous expansion of ecosystems, innovative solutions to risks and challenges, and unparalleled opportunities for early adopters. This chapter explores how DeFi is evolving, the hurdles it faces, and why it remains one of the most exciting opportunities for individuals and institutions alike.

DeFi is rapidly transitioning from niche adoption to mainstream integration, fueled by the expansion of its ecosystems. As the sector grows, it becomes increasingly interconnected, with diverse protocols and platforms working together to create comprehensive financial systems. This interconnectedness enables users to access various services, from lending and borrowing to trading, staking, and insurance. DeFi altcoins are at the center of this expansion, acting as the building blocks that power these platforms and provide liquidity, governance, and utility.

The expansion of DeFi ecosystems is driven by innovation. Developers continually push the boundaries of what decentralized protocols can achieve, introducing new mechanisms and models that enhance efficiency and usability. For instance, advancements in automated market makers (AMMs) and liquidity pools have transformed decentralized exchanges, making trading more efficient and accessible. Similarly, innovations in collateralization models and yield optimization have improved the sustainability and profitability of lending platforms.

These developments not only attract more users but also create opportunities for the integration of traditional financial institutions into the DeFi space.

Interoperability is another critical factor in the expansion of DeFi ecosystems. Connecting multiple blockchain networks allows DeFi protocols to operate across different ecosystems, unlocking new levels of functionality and collaboration. Cross-chain bridges, for example, enable users to transfer assets between blockchains, creating a seamless experience that transcends the limitations of individual networks. This interoperability fosters a more cohesive and inclusive financial system where users can access the best features of multiple platforms without being constrained by silos.

However, the expansion of DeFi ecosystems has its challenges. The sector's rapid growth has exposed vulnerabilities and risks that must be addressed to ensure its long-term viability. Security remains one of the most significant concerns, as DeFi protocols are often targeted by hackers seeking to exploit vulnerabilities in smart contracts or underlying infrastructure. High-profile breaches and exploits have highlighted the need for rigorous auditing, robust development practices, and continuous monitoring to safeguard user funds and maintain trust.

Regulation is another pressing challenge for DeFi. The sector's decentralized nature often places it outside the purview of traditional regulatory frameworks, creating uncertainty for users and developers. Governments and regulatory bodies are increasingly scrutinizing DeFi, raising questions about compliance, taxation, and consumer protection. While regulation can provide legitimacy and stability, overly restrictive policies could stifle innovation and limit the sector's potential. Striking the right balance between regulation and decentralization will be crucial for DeFi's future.

Market volatility poses additional risks for DeFi. Cryptocurrencies, the primary assets used in DeFi protocols, are inherently volatile, and sudden price fluctuations can have cascading effects on the ecosystem. For instance, a sharp decline in the value of collateral can trigger liquidations, leading to instability in lending platforms and liquidity pools. Addressing these risks requires the development of more robust risk management mechanisms, such as dynamic collateralization ratios and insurance protocols that protect users from unexpected losses.

Despite these challenges, the future of DeFi is filled with opportunities, particularly for early adopters. Those who recognize the potential of DeFi altcoins and protocols early on can position themselves to benefit from the sector's growth. Early adopters have the advantage of participating in the development and governance of DeFi platforms, often receiving rewards in the form of tokens or yields. These rewards can provide significant returns as the platforms gain traction and their native tokens appreciate in value.

One of the most compelling opportunities for early adopters is the chance to shape the direction of DeFi. Governance tokens, a common feature of DeFi protocols, enable users to vote on key decisions, such as protocol upgrades, fee structures, and resource allocation. By participating in governance, early adopters can influence the evolution of DeFi platforms and ensure that they align with the needs and priorities of their communities. This participatory model reflects the decentralized ethos of DeFi and empowers users to take an active role in shaping the future of finance.

Another key opportunity offered by DeFi is the democratization of finance. Traditional financial systems often exclude individuals who need access to banks, credit, or investment opportunities, particularly in developing regions. DeFi removes these barriers, allowing anyone with an internet connection and a digital wallet to participate in global financial markets. This inclusivity empowers individuals and creates new markets and revenue streams, driving economic growth and innovation.

DeFi also offers opportunities for institutions seeking to modernize their operations and explore new revenue models. Financial institutions can leverage DeFi protocols to streamline processes, reduce costs, and access new liquidity pools. For example, banks can use DeFi lending platforms to provide loans without the overhead of traditional methods, while asset managers can optimize their portfolios using DeFi yield strategies. These integrations demonstrate how DeFi can complement and enhance conventional financial systems, creating a more efficient and interconnected financial ecosystem.

As DeFi continues to evolve, its potential to disrupt traditional finance becomes increasingly apparent. The sector's ability to provide transparent, efficient, and accessible financial services positions it as a powerful alternative to centralized systems. However, realizing this potential requires addressing rapid growth's risks and challenges. Security, regulation, and market volatility must be managed carefully to ensure the stability and sustainability of DeFi ecosystems.

The opportunities for early adopters in DeFi are vast, ranging from financial rewards to the chance to shape the future of finance. By participating in DeFi protocols and investing in DeFi altcoins, individuals and institutions can play a pivotal role in the development of a decentralized financial system that is more inclusive, innovative, and resilient than ever before. The future of DeFi is not just about technology; it is about transforming how we think about and interact with money, creating a world where financial opportunities are accessible to all.

# CHAPTER 4: GAMING AND METAVERSE ALTCOINS

*"The metaverse is the next evolution of social connection and the successor to the mobile internet."* — Mark Zuckerberg.

Zuckerberg's vision for the metaverse speaks to the profound shift in how we connect, interact, and engage in digital spaces. Gaming and metaverse altcoins are at the forefront of this transformation, enabling decentralized economies where users truly own their digital assets. Unlike traditional online platforms, which centralize control and ownership, blockchain-based metaverse projects empower individuals to create, trade, and profit within virtual environments.

These altcoins facilitate the creation of immersive worlds where economic activity thrives. For example, platforms like Decentraland allow users to buy, sell, and develop virtual real estate, creating a new frontier for investment and creativity. Play-to-earn models, powered by altcoins such as Axie Infinity, reward players for their engagement, blurring the lines between work and entertainment. The metaverse also redefines social interactions. By integrating blockchain technology, users can maintain their digital identities across multiple platforms, fostering continuity and community. The decentralized nature of these ecosystems ensures that no single entity has control, promoting inclusivity and innovation.

Zuckerberg's statement highlights how the metaverse represents the next stage in digital evolution, much like how the mobile internet revolutionized communication and commerce. Gaming and metaverse altcoins are the building blocks of this new era, creating dynamic ecosystems where technology, economy, and society intersect in unprecedented ways.

The integration of blockchain technology into gaming has sparked a revolutionary wave within the industry. This transformation has given birth to innovative models, reshaping how players interact with games, digital assets, and each other. Gaming and metaverse altcoins are at the heart of this revolution, which provides the infrastructure and incentives for a new era of decentralized, player-driven ecosystems.

Blockchain gaming has emerged as a novel frontier in entertainment and finance, offering the unique benefits of true ownership of in-game assets, facilitating decentralized economies, and introducing Play-to-Earn (P2E) models.

Blockchain gaming represents a paradigm shift, merging the worlds of gaming and cryptocurrency to create experiences where players are not just participants but stakeholders in the ecosystem. This shift from centralized gaming economies to decentralized ones empowers players, giving them control over their assets and the rules governing the game. It's a transformation that inspires and motivates, as it allows players to derive real-world value from their virtual activities.

In blockchain-based games, in-game items, characters, and currencies are often represented as non-fungible tokens (NFTs) or fungible tokens on decentralized networks. These tokens are recorded on a blockchain, providing verifiable proof of ownership and allowing players to transfer them between wallets, trade them on marketplaces, or use them across multiple games. This level of interoperability and ownership is unprecedented, empowering players to derive real-world value from their virtual activities.

Play-to-earn (P2E) models have become one of the most significant innovations in blockchain gaming. P2E games reward players with cryptocurrency or NFTs for their participation, turning gaming into a potentially lucrative endeavor. This model aligns the interests of developers and players, as both benefit from the growth and success of the ecosystem. For developers,

P2E incentivizes player engagement and retention. In contrast, players gain financial rewards and a sense of ownership in the game's economy.

Play-to-earn (P2E) has garnered significant attention in regions with limited traditional economic opportunities. For example, in countries like the Philippines, games like Axie Infinity have become a source of income for thousands of players. By participating in battles, completing quests, or breeding digital pets, players earn cryptocurrency that can be converted into fiat currency or reinvested in the game. This economic model has given rise to a new generation of 'crypto gamers' who view gaming as a pastime and a viable source of income. It's an intriguing and exciting concept, turning gaming into a potentially lucrative endeavor.

Gamers' adoption of blockchain technology has been driven by several factors, including the growing awareness of cryptocurrency and the desire for more equitable gaming ecosystems. Gamers are often early adopters of new technologies, making them a natural audience for blockchain innovation. Many players have expressed frustration with the centralized control exerted by traditional game publishers, who can devalue assets, shut down servers, or restrict access to content at their discretion. Blockchain gaming addresses these concerns by creating decentralized systems where players have greater control over their assets and game rules.

The rise of esports and live streaming has also contributed to the adoption of blockchain in gaming. Competitive gaming and content creation have become lucrative industries, with professional players and streamers earning substantial incomes through sponsorships, advertisements, and viewer donations. Blockchain technology enhances these opportunities by enabling direct monetization and creating new revenue streams. For instance, streamers can mint their exclusive content as NFTs, allowing fans to own unique digital memorabilia. Similarly, esports organizations can issue tokens, allowing fans to invest in and support their favorite teams.

NFT integration in games represents another groundbreaking development in blockchain gaming. Non-fungible tokens allow developers to create unique, verifiable assets that players can own, trade, or use within games. These assets can take various forms, such as weapons, skins, virtual land, or characters, each with distinct attributes and value. By integrating NFTs, games create decentralized economies where players drive demand and value through actions and interactions.

One of the most compelling use cases for NFTs in gaming is virtual land ownership. In metaverse platforms like Decentraland and The Sandbox, players can purchase and own virtual real estate, represented as NFTs. These virtual plots can be customized, monetized, or used as spaces for social interaction, creating a new dimension of engagement. Virtual land ownership has attracted gamers, artists, brands, and investors who see the potential for creativity, community building, and profit within these digital worlds.

NFTs enable cross-game interoperability, allowing

players to use their assets across multiple games or platforms. For example, a player might purchase a sword in one game and use it as a weapon in another or display it as a collectible in their virtual home. This level of integration creates a cohesive gaming experience and expands the utility of NFTs, driving their adoption and value.

However, the integration of NFTs in games has been subject to controversy. Critics have raised concerns about the environmental impact of blockchain technology, particularly for platforms that rely on energy-intensive proof-of-work (PoW) consensus mechanisms. Developers and players have also expressed apprehension about the speculative nature of NFTs, fearing that gaming could become overly commercialized or exploitative. These challenges highlight the need for sustainable and ethical practices in blockchain gaming to ensure its long-term success and acceptance.

Despite the concerns, the potential of blockchain gaming and metaverse altcoins is vast. They are not just transforming, but reshaping the gaming industry by introducing new economic models, fostering community-driven development, and enabling true ownership of digital assets. As the technology matures, we can expect to see even more innovative applications and use cases, further blurring the lines between gaming, finance, and social interaction.

Integrating blockchain in gaming also has implications for the broader metaverse. Users can interact, create, and transact in this collective virtual space. Metaverse altcoins are crucial in enabling these interactions by providing the infrastructure for decentralized economies and digital identities. By combining gaming, social networking, and commerce, the metaverse represents a convergence of industries that could redefine how we engage with technology and each other. It's a concept that fosters a sense of community, making users feel connected and engaged in this collective virtual space.

Gaming and metaverse altcoins are leading this transformation, showcasing the power of blockchain technology to create more equitable, immersive, and rewarding digital experiences. As the gaming industry evolves, these altcoins will play an increasingly pivotal role in shaping its future, offering players and developers new ways to connect, collaborate, and thrive in a decentralized world. This fusion of gaming and blockchain is not just a trend but a glimpse into the future of entertainment and digital economies.

**Metaverse Expansion with Altcoins**
The metaverse, a shared virtual reality where people can interact, socialize, create, and transact, represents one of the most ambitious technological endeavors of the 21st century. It is a digital universe powered by blockchain technology, where altcoins play a foundational role in building virtual economies and enabling new forms of ownership and digital identity. As the concept of the metaverse expands, altcoins are becoming essential to its infrastructure, driving innovation and unlocking possibilities that were once limited to science fiction.

At its core, the metaverse is a collection of interconnected virtual worlds where users can participate in activities ranging from gaming and social networking to commerce and creative expression. These virtual worlds are not merely simulations; they are living, breathing economies driven by their participants' contributions. Blockchain technology underpins this ecosystem, providing the tools to establish trust, transparency, and decentralization. Altcoins serve as the lifeblood of these virtual worlds, facilitating transactions, incentivizing participation, and enabling governance.

Building virtual worlds in the metaverse requires a robust and scalable infrastructure supporting various activities and interactions. Unlike traditional online platforms controlled by centralized entities, metaverse platforms are increasingly adopting decentralized architectures powered by blockchain technology. This shift allows users to play a more active role in shaping the virtual environments they inhabit. Through decentralized governance, participants can vote on changes, propose new features, and contribute to the development of the metaverse. Altcoins enable this participatory model by allowing users to stake their tokens, cast votes, and earn rewards for their contributions.

Virtual worlds in the metaverse are often composed of parcels of digital land, represented as non-fungible tokens (NFTs) on the blockchain. Users can purchase, own, and trade these parcels, creating a decentralized real estate market within the metaverse. Ownership of virtual land allows users to build and customize their environments, turning them into gaming, socializing, commerce, or artistic expression spaces. This level of creative freedom fosters innovation and collaboration as users experiment with new ways to interact and engage within the metaverse.

Altcoins are crucial in powering metaverse economies by serving as the primary medium of exchange and value within these virtual worlds. Transactions involving virtual land, digital assets, and services use native tokens specific to each metaverse platform. For example, Decentraland uses MANA as its currency, while The Sandbox relies on SAND. These tokens facilitate commerce and incentivize users to participate in the ecosystem. For instance, users can earn tokens by creating content, hosting events, or providing services within the metaverse, turning their contributions into tangible rewards.

The economic potential of the metaverse extends beyond individual transactions. Entire industries are emerging within virtual worlds, driven by the creativity and entrepreneurship of their participants. Digital fashion is an industry where designers create and sell virtual clothing and accessories for avatars. These items, often minted as NFTs, can be traded or displayed across multiple platforms, showcasing the interoperability and value of blockchain assets. Similarly, virtual events such as concerts, art exhibitions, and conferences have become lucrative enterprises, attracting audiences from around the globe and generating revenue through ticket sales, sponsorships, and merchandise.

Ownership in the metaverse fundamentally differs from traditional notions of property. In the physical world, legal frameworks, geographic boundaries, and material constraints often limit ownership. In the metaverse, ownership is defined by blockchain technology, which provides a secure and verifiable record of who owns what. This digital ledger ensures that users have true control over their assets, whether virtual land, collectibles, or currencies. Unlike traditional online platforms, where assets are often tied to a centralized account and subject to the provider's terms of service, blockchain-based ownership gives users the freedom to transfer, trade, or utilize their assets as they see fit.

Ownership in the metaverse is closely tied to the concept of digital identity. As users navigate virtual worlds, their digital identity becomes critical to their interactions and experiences. Blockchain technology enables the creation of decentralized digital identities, which are not controlled by any single entity but instead owned and managed by the user. These identities can be linked to assets, achievements, and reputation, creating a rich and persistent profile that reflects the user's presence in the metaverse.

Altcoins are pivotal in supporting digital identities by enabling trustless authentication and verification. For instance, users can prove their ownership of an NFT or token without revealing sensitive personal information, ensuring privacy and security in their interactions. This capability is particularly important in the metaverse, where anonymity and pseudonymity are often valued. At the same time, digital identities can build trust and foster community as users accumulate credentials and reputations that are verifiable on the blockchain.

The expansion of the metaverse is also transforming how we think about value creation and distribution. Traditional economies are often hierarchical, with wealth and power concentrated in the hands of a few entities. In contrast, metaverse economies are inherently decentralized, with value distributed among participants based on their contributions. This democratization of opportunity is one of the most compelling aspects of the metaverse, as it allows individuals to monetize their creativity, skills, and time in previously unimaginable ways.

Despite its promise, the metaverse faces several challenges as it expands. Scalability is a major concern, as the infrastructure needed to support millions of users and transactions is still in its early stages of development. Blockchain networks must evolve to handle the demands of metaverse platforms, ensuring fast, efficient, and secure interactions. Interoperability is another critical issue, as the metaverse will only reach its full potential if users can move seamlessly between virtual worlds and carry their assets and identities with them.

Regulation and governance also present challenges for the metaverse. As the line between the physical and virtual worlds blurs, questions arise about how these spaces should be governed and who should enforce the rules. Decentralized governance models offer a potential solution but require careful design and implementation to ensure fairness, inclusivity, and transparency. Additionally, regulators are beginning to scrutinize the metaverse, raising questions about taxation, intellectual property, and consumer protection. Balancing the need for regulation with the principles of decentralization will be crucial for the metaverse to thrive.

Altcoins are poised to play an increasingly important role in addressing these challenges and driving the expansion of the metaverse. They provide the economic and technological foundation for building virtual worlds, powering decentralized economies, and enabling ownership and digital identity. As the metaverse grows, altcoins will continue to evolve, offering new capabilities and use cases that push the boundaries of what is possible in virtual spaces.

The metaverse represents a convergence of gaming, social networking, commerce, and creativity, creating a new paradigm for interacting with technology and each other. Altcoins are at the heart of this transformation, empowering users to shape their digital experiences and participate in a decentralized economy. As the metaverse expands, it will redefine not only entertainment and business but also fundamental concepts of identity, ownership, and community. The journey into the metaverse is just beginning, and altcoins are lighting the way forward.

## Notable Gaming And Metaverse Altcoins

Blockchain technology has paved the way for a new era in gaming and virtual worlds, where players and creators can participate in decentralized economies and shape immersive digital spaces. Gaming and metaverse altcoins are at the heart of this transformation, which provides the infrastructure and incentives for these dynamic ecosystems. Among the most notable are Axie Infinity, Decentraland, and Gala Games, each of which exemplifies the unique potential of blockchain technology to revolutionize gaming, ownership, and interaction in the virtual realm.

Axie Infinity has become a symbol of the Play-to-Earn (P2E) revolution, demonstrating how blockchain gaming can empower individuals to earn real-world income through their virtual activities. Developed by Sky Mavis, Axie Infinity allows players to breed, trade, and battle digital creatures known as Axies. Each Axie is represented as a non-fungible token (NFT) on the blockchain, ensuring that players have verifiable ownership of their assets. The game's economy is driven by its native tokens, Axie Infinity Shards (AXS) and Smooth Love Potion (SLP), which can be earned through gameplay and traded on various platforms.

The success of Axie Infinity lies in its innovative approach to combining gaming and finance. Unlike traditional games, where in-game assets hold no value outside the platform, Axie Infinity enables players to monetize their efforts and creativity. By participating in battles, completing daily tasks, and breeding Axies, players earn SLP, which can be exchanged for fiat currency or used within the game to unlock additional opportunities. This economic model has transformed gaming from a leisure activity into a viable source of income, particularly in regions with limited traditional employment opportunities.

In countries like the Philippines, Axie Infinity has created a phenomenon where players earn more through the game than they might in conventional jobs.

This economic empowerment has attracted millions of users, fostering a vibrant and engaged community. The AXS token adds another layer of utility by enabling governance and staking, giving players a voice in the game's development and allowing them to earn rewards for their long-term commitment.

Despite its popularity, Axie Infinity has faced challenges, including the volatility of its token prices and the need to balance its economy. Maintaining a sustainable ecosystem requires careful token issuance, rewards, and player growth management. The team behind Axie Infinity has introduced measures such as dynamic reward systems and improved gameplay mechanics to address these issues. These efforts highlight the complexity of building and maintaining a decentralized gaming economy but also underscore the potential of P2E models to redefine how we think about gaming and work.

While Axie Infinity focuses on gameplay-driven economies, Decentraland takes a different approach by creating a decentralized platform for virtual real estate and social interaction. Decentraland is built on the Ethereum blockchain and allows users to buy, sell, and develop parcels of virtual land represented as NFTs. These parcels form the foundation of a digital world where players can build environments, host events, and create experiences that attract other users.

The appeal of Decentraland lies in its emphasis on ownership and creativity. By purchasing virtual land, users can shape their digital spaces into galleries, shops, concert venues, or even virtual offices. This level of customization has attracted artists, brands, and entrepreneurs, who see Decentraland as a platform for engaging with audiences in new and innovative ways. The platform's native token, MANA, serves as the currency for purchasing land, goods, and services within the ecosystem and participating in governance.

Decentraland's economy extends beyond virtual real estate. The platform has become a hub for events, entertainment, and commerce, hosting everything from art exhibitions to virtual fashion shows. These activities allow users to monetize their creativity and build communities around shared interests. Blockchain technology ensures that ownership and transactions are secure and transparent, fostering trust among participants.

The potential of Decentraland has not gone unnoticed by major companies and institutions. Several high-profile brands have entered the platform, using it to create immersive experiences and connect with tech-savvy audiences. This adoption highlights the growing recognition of virtual worlds as a valuable marketing and engagement tool and their potential to complement traditional business models.

However, Decentraland needs help with scaling and user retention. Building a compelling virtual world requires robust technology and a consistent influx of engaging content and activities. To address this, Decentraland has focused on enhancing its tools for creators, offering resources and incentives to encourage innovation. The platform's decentralized governance model, powered by MANA holders, allows the community to shape its development and ensure it remains aligned with user interests.

Gala Games takes a broader approach to blockchain gaming by building an ecosystem that supports multiple games and developers. Founded by Eric Schiermeyer, one of the co-founders of Zynga, Gala Games aims to empower players and creators by giving them ownership of in-game assets and control over the direction of their favorite games. Unlike single-game platforms, Gala Games provides a decentralized infrastructure that can host various games, each with its own unique economy and mechanics.

At the heart of the Gala Games ecosystem is the GALA token, which serves as the primary currency for transactions and governance. Players can earn GALA through gameplay, participate in game-specific economies, and use the token to purchase NFTs and other in-game items. The token also gives users a say in the platform's development, creating a collaborative environment where players and developers work together to build the ecosystem.

Gala Games has attracted attention for its emphasis on community-driven development. By leveraging blockchain technology, the platform ensures that players have true ownership of their assets and a voice in shaping the games they play. This approach aligns with the principles of decentralization and transparency, fostering user trust and engagement. The platform's success is evident in its growing library of games, which spans genres such as strategy, role-playing, and simulation.

One of Gala Games' most notable achievements is its integration of NFTs into gameplay. These NFTs represent unique items, characters, or abilities players can use, trade, or display across the ecosystem. The interoperability of these assets creates a cohesive gaming experience and adds value to the ecosystem. Gala Games has also partnered with developers and creators to expand its offerings, ensuring a steady stream of new and exciting content for players.

Despite its promise, Gala Games needs help maintaining its momentum and scaling its operations. Building a successful gaming ecosystem requires balancing the needs of developers, players, and investors and navigating the complexities of blockchain technology. Gala Games has focused on addressing these challenges through innovation, collaboration, and community engagement, positioning itself as a leader in the blockchain gaming space.

The rise of Axie Infinity, Decentraland, and Gala Games underscores the transformative potential of gaming and metaverse altcoins. Each project highlights a different aspect of what is possible with blockchain technology, from P2E models and virtual real estate to decentralized ecosystems and creative ownership. Together, they represent a new gaming and virtual interaction era, where players and creators are empowered to shape their experiences and participate in decentralized economies.

As the gaming and metaverse industries evolve, these altcoins will be critical in driving innovation, fostering community, and expanding user opportunities worldwide. Their success demonstrates the viability of blockchain technology in entertainment. It paves the way for a future where virtual worlds and decentralized economies are integral parts of our lives. These projects are just the beginning of what is possible, and their impact will continue to shape the landscape of gaming and the metaverse for years to come.

# CHAPTER 5: PRIVACY-FOCUSED ALTCOINS

*"Privacy is not an option, and it shouldn't be the price we accept for just getting on the Internet."* — Gary Kovacs.

Kovacs's statement underscores the growing importance of privacy in the digital age, where personal data has become a valuable commodity. Privacy-focused altcoins directly address this issue by offering secure and anonymous transactions, empowering users to protect their information and maintain control over their digital identities. As the world becomes increasingly interconnected, the need for privacy in financial and online interactions is more critical than ever.

Blockchain technology, by its nature, provides transparency, but this can sometimes compromise individual privacy. Privacy-focused altcoins like Monero, Zcash, and Secret Network have developed advanced protocols to balance transparency with confidentiality. These projects enable transactions that are both verifiable and untraceable, protecting sensitive information from public exposure. By prioritizing user privacy, these altcoins ensure that financial autonomy is preserved without sacrificing security.

In an era where data breaches, identity theft, and intrusive surveillance are rampant, privacy-focused altcoins represent a counterbalance to centralized systems that exploit personal information. They empower individuals to reclaim control over their digital presence, fostering trust and confidence in decentralized systems. Kovacs's observation highlights the fundamental need for privacy as a right, not a privilege. By leveraging innovative technologies to safeguard anonymity, privacy-focused altcoins set a precedent for ethical and secure interactions in the digital economy.

◆ ◆ ◆

In the age of digital finance, where blockchain technology has introduced unprecedented transparency and accessibility, the importance of privacy has become a critical consideration. Privacy-focused altcoins have emerged as a powerful solution to address concerns about exposing sensitive financial information on public blockchains. These cryptocurrencies are not just designed to protect user anonymity and enhance the confidentiality of transactions, but also to empower individuals and businesses that value privacy in an increasingly surveilled digital world. Understanding the need for privacy in crypto, the challenges it addresses, and the regulatory complexities surrounding privacy coins sheds light on their significance and future in the blockchain ecosystem, providing a sense of control and security.

The advent of blockchain technology brought with it the promise of decentralized and transparent financial systems. While these attributes have transformed industries and empowered users, they have also exposed a significant vulnerability: the lack of privacy. Traditional blockchain networks like Bitcoin and Ethereum record every transaction on a public ledger accessible to anyone. Although these transactions do not directly reveal personal information, they are pseudonymous, meaning that a user's wallet address is visible and can potentially be linked to their real-world identity through blockchain analysis.

The need for privacy in cryptocurrency transactions arises from several factors. First, financial information is inherently sensitive. Whether it is a personal purchase, a salary payment, or a business transaction, exposing this data can lead to various risks, including identity theft, financial fraud, and loss of competitive advantage. For individuals, the lack of privacy can result in unwanted scrutiny or harassment, particularly for high-profile users whose financial activities might attract attention. For businesses, it can jeopardize confidential dealings, reveal supply chain relationships, or expose sensitive pricing strategies.

Another compelling reason for privacy in crypto is the

growing prevalence of surveillance and data collection in the digital age. Governments, corporations, and malicious actors increasingly leverage technology to track and monitor online activities, including financial transactions. While these measures are often justified as necessary for combating illicit activities, they also infringe on the privacy rights of law-abiding citizens. Privacy-focused altcoins safeguard against such intrusions, enabling users to maintain control over their financial information and assert their right to privacy.

Blockchain technology, despite its many advantages, inherently lacks privacy. The public nature of most blockchains means that every transaction is recorded and stored indefinitely, creating a permanent and transparent record of financial activity. While valuable for ensuring trust and accountability, this transparency also makes blockchain networks susceptible to privacy breaches. Advanced analytics tools and techniques allow entities to trace transactions, link addresses, and infer relationships, undermining the pseudonymity of traditional blockchains.

Privacy concerns in blockchain are not limited to individuals. Businesses and organizations that adopt blockchain technology face similar risks as their financial operations become more visible to competitors, regulators, and other stakeholders. This lack of confidentiality can deter adoption and limit blockchain's potential to transform industries such as finance, healthcare, and supply chain management. Privacy-focused altcoins address these challenges by introducing features that obscure transaction details, protect user identities, and enhance data confidentiality.

The technological innovations behind privacy-focused altcoins are designed to provide robust privacy protections without sacrificing the benefits of decentralization and security. Techniques such as zero-knowledge proofs, ring signatures, and stealth addresses enable users to conduct transactions without revealing sensitive information. Zero-knowledge proofs allow one party to prove to another that a statement is true without disclosing any underlying data. This approach ensures that transactions are verified without exposing the sender, recipient, or transaction amount.

Ring signatures, used by altcoins like Monero, mix a user's transaction with those of others, making it difficult to trace the origin of funds. On the other hand, stealth addresses generate unique one-time addresses for each transaction, ensuring that a recipient's identity remains hidden even if their wallet address is known. These techniques, combined with encryption and other privacy-enhancing measures, create a level of confidentiality that is unattainable on traditional blockchains.

Privacy-focused altcoins have many use cases that extend beyond individual transactions. For businesses, they offer a way to protect sensitive financial information, enabling secure and confidential dealings. Companies can use privacy coins to pay suppliers, manage payroll, or execute strategic transactions without revealing details to competitors or unauthorized parties. This confidentiality is particularly valuable in industries where discretion is critical, such as pharmaceuticals, defense, and mergers and acquisitions.

For individuals, privacy-focused altcoins provide a means to safeguard personal financial data in an era of increasing digital surveillance. They enable users to make purchases, transfer funds, and manage investments without fear of tracking or exploiting their activities. More than just a tool for personal privacy, privacy coins play a significant role in protecting civil liberties, especially in regions where financial censorship, authoritarian regimes, or economic instability threaten the ability of citizens to access and use money freely, fostering a sense of connection to the broader social impact of these technologies.

Another significant use case is the role of privacy coins in humanitarian efforts and social activism. In areas affected by conflict, repression, or natural disasters, these coins can facilitate the secure transfer of aid and support to vulnerable populations without exposing recipients to additional risks. Privacy coins empower individuals and organizations to navigate complex and sensitive situations, preserving confidentiality and ensuring the integrity of their efforts. This potential for positive impact in humanitarian and social causes can inspire the audience about the broader implications of these technologies.

Despite their many benefits, privacy-focused altcoins face considerable regulatory challenges. Governments and regulatory bodies have expressed concerns about their potential misuse of illegal activities such as money laundering, tax evasion, and financing terrorism. The anonymity provided by privacy coins makes them an attractive option for criminals seeking to hide their financial activities, creating a tension between the legitimate need for privacy and the imperative to prevent illicit behavior.

Several countries have introduced regulations or outright bans on privacy coins in response to these concerns. Exchanges in jurisdictions with stringent anti-money laundering (AML) and know-your-customer (KYC) requirements often delist privacy-focused altcoins to comply with regulatory mandates. This creates barriers to adoption and limits the availability of these coins to users who value privacy for legitimate reasons. The regulatory scrutiny of privacy coins also raises questions about their compatibility with emerging global financial transparency and compliance standards.

Balancing the need for privacy with regulatory requirements is a complex challenge that requires collaboration between developers, regulators, and users. Privacy-focused altcoins must demonstrate their commitment to ethical and lawful use while preserving the principles of decentralization and individual empowerment. Innovations such as opt-in transparency, where users can choose to reveal transaction details to trusted parties, offer a potential solution. These features allow privacy coins to meet compliance requirements without compromising their core values.

The regulatory landscape for privacy coins is evolving, and their future will depend on how effectively they address the concerns of governments and institutions. Education and advocacy will be crucial in shaping public perception and policy, highlighting privacy-focused altcoins' legitimate use cases and benefits. By fostering dialogue and collaboration, the blockchain community can work toward a framework that supports privacy and compliance, ensuring that these coins remain valuable for individuals and businesses.

Privacy-focused altcoins represent a critical innovation in the cryptocurrency space, addressing the growing demand for confidentiality and security in a transparent digital economy. They offer solutions to the privacy concerns inherent in blockchain technology, enabling secure and anonymous transactions while empowering users to assert control over their financial data. Despite their challenges, privacy coins can transform how we think about privacy, trust, and security in the digital age.

As the blockchain ecosystem continues to evolve, the role of privacy-focused altcoins will become increasingly important. They provide a vital counterbalance to the transparency of traditional blockchains, ensuring that users can engage in financial activities without sacrificing their right to privacy. By navigating the complexities of regulation and fostering innovation, privacy coins can help build a more inclusive, secure, and equitable digital economy. Their journey reflects the broader struggle to balance transparency and privacy in a connected world, underscoring the importance of protecting individual freedoms in the face of technological advancement.

## Top Privacy Altcoins

Privacy-focused altcoins have emerged as a critical innovation in cryptocurrency, addressing the need for confidential transactions and secure data sharing in a digital economy increasingly shaped by transparency and surveillance. Among the most prominent privacy coins are Monero, Zcash, and Secret Network, each of which exemplifies unique approaches to protecting user anonymity while maintaining the functionality and utility of blockchain technology. These altcoins illustrate the diversity of privacy solutions available and their potential to reshape how individuals and organizations engage with digital finance and data.

Monero, often considered the gold standard for privacy coins, has established itself as a leader in advanced privacy protocols. Launched in 2014, Monero was designed with privacy as its primary focus, utilizing cutting-edge technologies to ensure that transactions remain confidential and untraceable. Unlike Bitcoin and other traditional cryptocurrencies, which rely on a transparent ledger, Monero obscures transaction details by default. This approach ensures that the sender, recipient, and transaction amount are shielded from public view, providing privacy unmatched by most other digital currencies.

One of the core technologies underpinning Monero's privacy is its use of ring signatures. Ring signatures allow a user's transaction to be mixed with multiple others, creating a layer of anonymity that makes it virtually impossible to trace the origin of funds. This mechanism ensures that every transaction on the Monero network is indistinguishable from the rest, preserving user privacy without requiring additional steps or actions. In addition to ring signatures, Monero employs stealth addresses, which generate unique, one-time addresses for each transaction. This feature prevents observers from linking a recipient's address to their transaction history, further enhancing confidentiality.

Monero also incorporates Ring Confidential Transactions (RingCT), a protocol that conceals transaction amounts. By hiding the exact values, RingCT ensures that even if a transaction is intercepted, the observer cannot determine how much was sent. These combined features make Monero a preferred choice for users who prioritize privacy, ranging from individuals concerned about financial surveillance to businesses seeking to protect sensitive data.

Despite its technological advancements, Monero faces challenges, particularly in the regulatory space. Its robust privacy features have drawn scrutiny from governments and regulators, who fear that such coins could be used for illicit activities. As a result, Monero has been delisted from several exchanges in jurisdictions with stringent anti-money laundering (AML) requirements. However, the Monero community has remained steadfast in its commitment to privacy, advocating for the coin's legitimate use cases and highlighting its potential to empower individuals in an increasingly surveilled world.

While Monero offers advanced privacy by default, Zcash takes a different approach by balancing privacy and transparency. Launched in 2016, Zcash was developed to provide users with the choice between transparent and private transactions. This dual functionality is enabled by its use of zk-SNARKs. This groundbreaking cryptographic technology allows users to prove the validity of a transaction without revealing any details about it. Zcash's ability to support transparent and shielded transactions has made it a versatile privacy coin, catering to a wide range of users and use cases.

Zcash's shielded transactions, which use zk-SNARKs, allow users to obscure the sender, recipient, and transaction amount while still ensuring the integrity of the network. This capability is particularly valuable for individuals and businesses that require privacy for specific transactions but are willing to operate transparently in other scenarios. By offering optional privacy, Zcash strikes a balance that appeals to privacy-conscious users and those needing to comply with regulatory requirements.

The flexibility of Zcash has contributed to its adoption across various sectors. For example, businesses can use Zcash to protect sensitive financial information, such as payroll data or supplier payments, while still maintaining transparency for regulatory purposes. Similarly, charities and non-profits can use Zcash to facilitate anonymous donations, preserving donor privacy while ensuring accountability for fund allocation. This adaptability has positioned Zcash as a leading privacy coin with broad applicability.

Despite its innovative approach, Zcash has faced challenges in achieving widespread adoption. The complexity of zk-SNARKs and the computational resources required to execute shielded transactions have been barriers for some users. However, ongoing developments aim to simplify the user experience and improve network efficiency, making Zcash more accessible to a broader audience. Additionally, the Zcash community and developers have been proactive in addressing regulatory concerns, working to educate policymakers about the legitimate use cases of privacy coins and their role in empowering users.

Secret Network takes privacy to another level by focusing on private smart contracts. This feature combines the confidentiality of privacy coins with the programmability of decentralized applications (dApps). Built on the Cosmos blockchain, Secret Network allows developers to create smart contracts that keep data encrypted and private, even during execution. This capability opens up new possibilities for privacy-preserving applications across various industries, from finance and healthcare to gaming and supply chain management.

Secret Network's privacy foundation lies in its use of secure enclaves. This hardware-based technology enables the encryption of data during processing. These enclaves ensure that sensitive information remains confidential, even as it is used within smart contracts. By enabling private computation, Secret Network addresses a critical limitation of traditional blockchains, where all data is visible to every participant in the network. This feature is particularly valuable for applications that handle sensitive information, such as medical records, financial transactions, or intellectual property.

Secret Network's native token, SCRT, plays a central role in its ecosystem, facilitating transactions, governance, and staking. The network's decentralized governance model allows SCRT holders to vote on proposals, ensuring the community has a say in the platform's development and direction. This participatory approach aligns with the principles of decentralization and transparency while preserving the privacy of individual users and transactions.

One of Secret Network's most compelling use cases is its ability to enable privacy in decentralized finance (DeFi). Traditional DeFi platforms often lack privacy features, exposing user activity to public scrutiny and creating vulnerabilities for front-running and other malicious activities. By integrating private smart contracts, Secret Network enhances the security and usability of DeFi applications, allowing users to interact with financial protocols without compromising their confidentiality.

The potential of Secret Network extends beyond DeFi. In gaming, private smart contracts enable the creation of secure and fair environments where players can participate without revealing their strategies or personal information. In supply chain management, the technology allows businesses to share critical data with partners while maintaining control over what is disclosed. These applications highlight the versatility of Secret Network and its ability to address privacy concerns across diverse sectors.

Despite its promise, Secret Network needs help gaining traction and building a robust ecosystem. As a relatively new player in the blockchain space, it must compete with established platforms and navigate the complexities of scaling its technology. However, the network's focus on privacy as a core feature sets it apart and positions it as a leader in the next wave of blockchain innovation.

Monero, Zcash, and Secret Network exemplify the diverse approaches to privacy in the cryptocurrency space. Each project addresses unique challenges and opportunities, from Monero's advanced protocols for untraceable transactions to Zcash's balance of privacy and transparency to Secret Network's groundbreaking private smart contracts. Together, these altcoins highlight the importance of privacy in a digital economy and demonstrate the transformative potential of blockchain technology to empower individuals and organizations.

As privacy concerns continue to grow in an interconnected world, the role of privacy-focused altcoins will become increasingly significant. They provide:

*-Critical tools for protecting sensitive information.*

*-Enabling secure interactions.*

*-Fostering trust in decentralized systems.*

By addressing the challenges of transparency and surveillance, these altcoins are paving the way for a more equitable and secure digital future in which privacy is not a luxury but a fundamental right.

## Challenges For Privacy Coins

Privacy coins have carved out a critical niche in the cryptocurrency landscape, addressing the growing demand for confidential transactions and the safeguarding of personal and financial data. These coins leverage advanced cryptographic technologies to give users greater privacy control. Still, their unique attributes also present significant challenges. From navigating regulatory scrutiny to overcoming technical hurdles, privacy coins face complex issues that influence their adoption and long-term viability. Balancing privacy and compliance, resolving scalability challenges, and building trust with stakeholders is pivotal in addressing these concerns and ensuring the sustainable growth of privacy-focused cryptocurrencies.

One of the most significant challenges for privacy coins is balancing the fundamental ethos of user anonymity with the need for regulatory compliance. Privacy coins are often at odds with the increasing global emphasis on transparency in financial systems. Governments and regulatory bodies worldwide have introduced stringent anti-money laundering (AML) and know-your-customer (KYC) requirements to combat financial crimes such as money laundering, tax evasion, and terrorism financing. Privacy coins, by design, offer transaction confidentiality, which can make it challenging for regulatory agencies to monitor illicit activities. This conflict has led to heightened scrutiny of privacy coins, with several jurisdictions imposing bans or restrictions on their use.

Exchanges, the primary on-ramps and off-ramps for cryptocurrency trading, have felt the brunt of regulatory pressure. Many have delisted privacy coins to comply with local laws, limiting their accessibility to users. This creates a significant barrier for privacy coins, as reduced availability can hinder adoption and liquidity. Privacy-focused cryptocurrencies must find ways to operate within regulatory frameworks without compromising their commitment to user privacy. This requires innovation in creating tools and mechanisms that allow for selective transparency, where users can disclose transaction details to authorized parties when necessary while still maintaining confidentiality for others.

The issue of compliance is particularly challenging because it varies across jurisdictions. What is acceptable in one country may be deemed illegal in another, creating a fragmented landscape for privacy coins. For developers and communities behind these cryptocurrencies, navigating this patchwork of regulations demands a delicate balance between adhering to local laws and upholding the principles of decentralization and privacy. Proactive engagement with regulators and educational efforts to highlight the legitimate use cases of privacy coins can help address misconceptions and foster a more favorable regulatory environment.

Scalability is another critical challenge for privacy coins. Advanced cryptographic techniques that enable privacy, such as zero-knowledge proofs and ring signatures, often have significant computational and storage requirements. These requirements can limit transaction throughput, increase fees, and create delays, making it difficult for privacy coins to scale effectively. As blockchain networks grow and more users transact simultaneously, these scalability issues become more pronounced, potentially undermining the user experience and adoption.

Monero, for instance, uses ring signatures to mix transactions, but as the number of participants in the ring increases, so does the computational complexity. Similarly, Zcash's zk-SNARK technology is powerful for ensuring privacy but requires substantial resources to generate and verify proofs. These technical limitations pose a significant barrier to widespread adoption, particularly compared to non-privacy-focused cryptocurrencies that can process transactions more quickly and efficiently.

Addressing scalability requires innovation at both the protocol and infrastructure levels. Layer-2 solutions, such as off-chain transactions or state channels, can improve scalability while preserving privacy. These solutions enable transactions outside the main blockchain, reducing congestion and computational load. Additionally, advancements in cryptographic techniques, such as zk-STARKs, promise to enhance the efficiency of privacy protocols, making them more scalable and accessible. By investing in research and development, privacy coins can overcome these challenges and compete more effectively with mainstream cryptocurrencies.

Building trust with stakeholders is another essential challenge for privacy coins. Unlike traditional cryptocurrencies, privacy coins must gain the trust of a wide range of participants, including users, developers, businesses, and regulators. For users, trust hinges on the security and effectiveness of the privacy features. If vulnerabilities are discovered or exploited, it can erode confidence in the coin's ability to protect sensitive information. Regular audits, transparency in development processes, and prompt responses to security issues are critical for maintaining user trust.

Businesses considering integrating privacy coins into their operations face additional concerns, such as the reputational risks associated with perceived regulatory non-compliance or association with illicit activities. To address these concerns, privacy coins must demonstrate their legitimacy and utility beyond anonymity. Highlighting real-world use cases, such as protecting consumer data, enabling secure cross-border payments, and safeguarding financial sovereignty, can help dispel misconceptions and encourage adoption by reputable organizations.

Regulators and policymakers are another key stakeholder group whose trust is vital for the long-term success of privacy coins. Building this trust requires proactive engagement, collaboration, and efforts to educate regulators about the legitimate use cases of privacy-focused cryptocurrencies. Demonstrating that privacy coins can coexist with regulatory frameworks, rather than undermining them, is essential for gaining acceptance and fostering a more supportive environment.

The decentralized nature of privacy coins adds another layer of complexity to trust-building efforts. Unlike traditional financial systems, where central authorities oversee compliance and risk management, privacy coins rely on their communities to govern and evolve. This decentralized governance model can create challenges in responding to regulatory changes or implementing new features. However, it also offers an opportunity to involve stakeholders directly in decision-making, fostering a sense of ownership and collaboration.

One of the most promising avenues for building trust is developing tools for selective transparency. These tools enable users to share transaction details with trusted parties, such as auditors, financial institutions, or regulators while maintaining privacy for others. By demonstrating a commitment to lawful use and accountability, privacy coins can address concerns about misuse without compromising their core values.

The challenges privacy coins face are not impossible but require a concerted effort. Balancing privacy and compliance, overcoming scalability issues, and building trust with stakeholders are interconnected challenges that demand innovation, collaboration, and a clear vision for the future. Privacy coins can transform digital finance by empowering individuals and businesses to protect sensitive information while participating in a decentralized economy. By navigating these challenges successfully, they can pave the way for a more secure, inclusive, and privacy-conscious financial ecosystem.

# CHAPTER 6: THE ROLE OF UTILITY ALTCOINS

*"The value of a token is directly related to the utility it provides." — Andreas M. Antonopoulos.*

Utility altcoins derive their value not from speculative trading but from the practical applications they enable. Antonopoulos's insight reflects how these tokens are integral to the functioning of blockchain ecosystems, powering services, applications, and operations that drive real-world use cases. Utility tokens are the backbone of blockchain innovation by enabling decentralized applications, facilitating transactions, and granting access to specific services.

Consider platforms like Ethereum, which introduced smart contracts powered by its native token, Ether. These contracts automate complex agreements without intermediaries, revolutionizing industries from finance to supply chain management. Similarly, Chainlink's LINK token facilitates secure data feeds for smart contracts, enabling them to interact with real-world information. These examples highlight how utility tokens extend blockchain's capabilities beyond currency to become essential components of decentralized systems.

Utility altcoins also incentivize user participation within their ecosystems. For instance, decentralized storage networks like Filecoin reward users who contribute storage space, creating a self-sustaining and decentralized infrastructure. This model fosters collaboration and innovation, ensuring that the ecosystem remains dynamic and effective. Antonopoulos's assertion emphasizes the importance of functionality in defining value. Utility altcoins are not just investments; they are tools that enable blockchain technology to address complex problems, improve efficiency, and create new opportunities across industries. Their practical relevance ensures their longevity and importance in the evolving digital landscape.

Utility altcoins represent one of the most dynamic and versatile categories of cryptocurrencies, acting as the lifeblood of blockchain ecosystems and decentralized networks. Unlike other cryptocurrencies that primarily serve as stores of value or mediums of exchange, utility coins are designed to provide specific functions within a network. They are integral to the operation of blockchain platforms, offering access, incentivizing participation, and powering ecosystems. As blockchain technology evolves, utility altcoins have become essential tools for enabling decentralized applications, services, and innovations.

The defining characteristic of utility coins is their functional purpose within a blockchain network. Rather than purely speculative assets, they give holders specific rights, access, or services. For example, some utility coins allow users to pay for transactions, access premium features, or participate in governance decisions. This functionality makes utility coins a cornerstone of blockchain networks, enabling them to operate efficiently and deliver value to their users.

Utility coins are often tied to decentralized applications (dApps) or platforms that rely on blockchain technology. These platforms span diverse industries, including finance, healthcare, gaming, and supply chain management. By integrating utility coins, developers create ecosystems where tokens facilitate interactions, incentivize user engagement, and sustain the network's growth. This integration ensures that utility coins are not just a speculative investment but a key driver of activity and innovation within their respective ecosystems.

The role of utility coins in providing network access is particularly significant. Many blockchain platforms require users to hold or use native utility coins to access services, execute transactions, or interact with applications. This requirement creates a direct link between the coin's value and the platform's utility, ensuring that the coin's success is tied to the growth and adoption of the network. For instance, platforms like Ethereum use utility coins to power smart contracts and pay transaction fees, making the coin an essential component of the network's functionality.

Utility coins also play a critical role in incentivizing participation within blockchain ecosystems. In decentralized networks, user participation is vital for maintaining security, scalability, and functionality. Utility coins often reward participants for their contributions, such as validating transactions, providing liquidity, or creating content. These incentives create a self-sustaining ecosystem where users are motivated to engage and contribute, driving the platform's growth and success.

Incentivization mechanisms powered by utility coins are particularly important in decentralized finance (DeFi) platforms. For example, users who provide liquidity to decentralized exchanges or participate in lending and borrowing protocols are often rewarded with utility coins. These rewards compensate users for their contributions and encourage them to remain active within the ecosystem. This dynamic creates a virtuous cycle where increased participation leads to greater network activity and, ultimately, higher utility for the coin.

The use of utility coins as incentives extends beyond financial applications. In gaming platforms, utility coins can be earned by completing quests, winning battles, or participating in tournaments. In social media networks, users might receive tokens for creating high-quality content or engaging with the community. These use cases highlight utility coins' versatility and ability to drive engagement across various sectors.

Another critical role of utility coins is powering blockchain ecosystems. These coins serve as the economic backbone of decentralized platforms, facilitating transactions, securing the network, and enabling governance. Utility coins create a cohesive ecosystem that supports innovation and growth by aligning the interests of users, developers, and stakeholders. In many blockchain networks, utility coins pay transaction fees, ensuring the network operates efficiently and securely. This fee model prevents spam attacks and incentivizes validators or miners to process transactions. By providing a clear economic incentive, utility coins ensure that the network remains functional and scalable even as it grows.

Utility coins also empower users in decentralized governance, giving them a voice in the decision-making processes of blockchain platforms. Governance tokens, a subset of utility coins, allow holders to propose and vote on changes to the protocol, such as fee structures, upgrades, or resource allocation. This participatory model ensures that the platform evolves in line with community needs and priorities, making users feel influential and involved.

The role of utility coins in governance is particularly significant in decentralized autonomous organizations (DAOs). These organizations rely on utility coins to manage operations, allocate resources, and make collective decisions. By distributing governance power among token holders, DAOs create a more inclusive and transparent model of decision-making that aligns with the principles of decentralization.

Utility coins also play a vital role in enabling cross-chain interoperability and collaboration. As blockchain ecosystems become more interconnected, utility coins facilitate seamless platform interactions, creating a unified and efficient network. For example, some utility coins bridge assets between blockchains, enabling users to transfer value and data across networks. This interoperability not only enhances the utility of blockchain technology but also expands the possibilities for innovation and integration, making the audience feel excited about the expanding possibilities in blockchain technology.

The success of utility coins is closely tied to the adoption and growth of their underlying platforms. As more users and developers join a network, the demand for its utility coin increases, driving its value and utility. This dynamic creates a positive feedback loop where the platform's growth and the utility coin's success are mutually reinforcing. However, this dependency also presents challenges, as the value of utility coins can be affected by factors such as competition, market sentiment, and technological developments.

Despite their potential, utility coins face several challenges that must be addressed to ensure their long-term success. One of the primary challenges is scalability. As blockchain networks grow, the demand for utility coins can outpace their supply, leading to congestion and high fees. Addressing these issues requires innovative solutions, such as layer-2 scaling (like the Lightning Network for Bitcoin or the Raiden Network for Ethereum), sharding (like the Zilliqa blockchain), or off-chain transactions (like the Bitcoin Lightning Network or Ethereum's Raiden Network), to enhance the efficiency and usability of utility coins.

Utility coins face another challenge of regulation, as their classification and treatment vary across jurisdictions. Some regulators view utility coins as securities, subjecting them to strict compliance requirements, while others classify them as commodities or payment tokens. Navigating this regulatory landscape, which includes compliance with anti-money laundering (AML) and know your customer (KYC) regulations, requires transparency, collaboration, and adherence to best practices to ensure that utility coins are compliant and accessible to users worldwide.

Utility coins have become indispensable tools for enabling decentralized networks and applications. Their role in providing network access, incentivizing participation, and powering ecosystems underscores their importance in blockchain. As technology evolves, utility coins will continue to play a central role in driving innovation, fostering engagement, and shaping the future of decentralized systems. By addressing their challenges and capitalizing on their potential, utility coins can unlock new possibilities for blockchain technology and redefine how we interact with digital platforms and services.

## Top Utility Coins In Action

Utility coins have revolutionized the blockchain ecosystem by offering more than just a store of value or a medium of exchange. These coins are the backbone for decentralized networks, providing access to services, incentivizing participation, and enabling innovative use cases. Among the most impactful utility coins are Chainlink, Filecoin, and Helium. Each represents a unique approach to leveraging blockchain technology, addressing distinct challenges, and unlocking new possibilities in Oracle solutions, decentralized storage, and IoT connectivity.

Chainlink has emerged as a leader in providing Oracle solutions, bridging the gap between blockchain networks and real-world data. Smart contracts, the cornerstone of decentralized applications (dApps), rely on accurate and timely data to execute their functions. However, blockchains are inherently isolated from external systems, creating a challenge for integrating off-chain information. Chainlink solves this problem by using its native utility token, LINK, to power a decentralized network of oracles that securely connect blockchains to external data sources, APIs, and payment systems.

Chainlink's role in the blockchain ecosystem cannot be overstated. Enabling smart contracts to access real-world data unlocks many use cases across industries. In decentralized finance (DeFi), for instance, Chainlink oracles provide price feeds for assets, enabling lending platforms, derivatives, and prediction markets to function accurately. In supply chain management, Chainlink enables the tracking and verifying of goods by integrating IoT data with blockchain records. This capability ensures transparency and authenticity in supply chain operations, reducing fraud and inefficiencies.

Chainlink's decentralized oracle network is powered by the LINK token, which incentivizes node operators to provide reliable and accurate data. Node operators stake LINK tokens as collateral, ensuring accountability and trustworthiness in the network. The token's utility extends beyond incentivizing operators; it also aligns the interests of participants and provides the system's integrity. As more smart contracts rely on Chainlink's oracles, the demand for LINK increases, driving its value and utility within the ecosystem.

Filecoin, another transformative utility coin, addresses the growing need for decentralized storage solutions. Data is one of the most valuable commodities in the digital age, yet traditional storage systems are centralized, expensive, and vulnerable to censorship and breaches. Filecoin provides a decentralized alternative by enabling users to rent out unused storage space on their devices, creating a distributed network for storing and retrieving data. The platform's native token, FIL, is central to this ecosystem, facilitating transactions between storage providers and users.

Filecoin's decentralized storage model offers several advantages over traditional systems. Distributing data across multiple nodes ensures redundancy and security, reducing the risk of data loss or tampering. The decentralized nature of the network also enhances privacy, as users retain control over their data without relying on centralized entities. Additionally, Filecoin's competitive marketplace incentivizes storage providers to offer affordable and efficient services, driving down user costs.

The FIL token is critical in the Filecoin network, serving as the currency for storage and retrieval transactions. Users pay FIL tokens to store their data, while providers earn tokens to offer storage space and maintain the network. This tokenized economy creates a self-sustaining system that rewards participants and ensures the network's functionality. Moreover, the token incentivizes long-term commitment, as providers must stake FIL tokens as collateral to guarantee the quality and reliability of their services.

Filecoin's applications extend beyond individual users to healthcare, finance, and media industries. For example, healthcare organizations can use Filecoin to store sensitive patient records securely, ensuring compliance with data protection regulations. Similarly, media companies can leverage the network to archive large volumes of content, reducing costs and enhancing accessibility. Filecoin is poised to play a vital role in the digital economy by providing a scalable and secure solution for data storage.

Helium offers a groundbreaking approach to IoT connectivity, leveraging blockchain technology and its native token, HNT, to create a decentralized wireless network. The Internet of Things (IoT) relies on efficient and reliable connectivity to enable devices to communicate and share data. Traditional IoT networks are often centralized, expensive, and limited in coverage. Helium addresses these challenges by building a decentralized network powered by individuals who deploy low-cost hardware devices called Hotspots.

Hotspots serve as nodes in the Helium network, providing wireless coverage for IoT devices while earning HNT tokens as rewards. This model incentivizes participation, creating a global network of interconnected nodes that offer low-power, long-range connectivity. By decentralizing IoT infrastructure, Helium reduces the barriers to entry for businesses and developers, enabling them to build and deploy IoT applications without relying on traditional network providers.

The utility of the HNT token is central to Helium's ecosystem. Device operators pay for network usage with Data Credits tied to HNT tokens. This dual-token model ensures that HNT retains value as the network grows while maintaining predictable costs for users. The token also aligns stakeholders' interests, incentivizing Hotspot owners to expand network coverage and improve service quality.

Helium's decentralized network has enabled many applications, from smart agriculture and asset tracking to environmental monitoring and logistics. For instance, farmers can use Helium-enabled sensors to monitor soil moisture and weather conditions, optimizing irrigation and improving crop yields. Logistics companies can deploy IoT trackers to monitor real-time shipments, enhancing efficiency and reducing losses. These use cases demonstrate the potential of Helium's decentralized model to transform industries and unlock new opportunities.

While Chainlink, Filecoin, and Helium each address unique challenges, they share a common thread in using utility coins to power decentralized networks. These coins are not merely speculative assets; they are integral to the functionality and sustainability of their respective platforms. Utility coins create ecosystems that foster innovation and engagement by providing incentives, enabling access, and driving participation.

The success of these utility coins highlights the transformative potential of blockchain technology to address real-world problems and create value across industries. Chainlink's Oracle solutions connect blockchains to external data, enabling smart contracts to interact with the physical world. Filecoin's decentralized storage network provides a secure and affordable alternative to traditional systems, empowering users to retain control over their data. Helium's decentralized IoT network reimagines connectivity, enabling businesses and developers to build the next generation of IoT applications.

As blockchain technology's adoption grows, utility coins' role will become increasingly significant. They serve as the economic and functional foundation of decentralized platforms, enabling them to operate efficiently and deliver value to their users. The success of Chainlink, Filecoin, and Helium demonstrates the versatility and impact of utility coins, paving the way for further innovation and integration in the blockchain ecosystem. These projects are not just examples of successful utility coins; they are harbingers of a future where decentralized networks power the digital economy and transform how we interact with technology and each other.

## Emerging Opportunities In Utility Tokens

Utility tokens represent one of cryptocurrency's most innovative and transformative elements. They enable many use cases and opportunities by providing functional value within blockchain ecosystems. While early utility tokens laid the foundation for decentralized platforms, the next generation unlocks even greater potential through tokenized services, community-driven growth, and enterprise partnerships. These emerging opportunities illustrate the growing relevance of utility tokens and their role in shaping the future of decentralized technology.

The concept of tokenized services is revolutionizing how businesses and individuals interact with digital platforms. At its core, tokenization involves converting access to services, rights, or assets into a digital token that can be seamlessly transferred and managed on a blockchain. This model enhances accessibility, efficiency, and transparency, making it a powerful tool for modernizing industries and creating new economic opportunities.

Tokenized services transform subscription-based models by enabling users to access products and services through utility tokens rather than traditional payment methods. This approach simplifies transactions and provides users with greater flexibility. For example, instead of subscribing to a streaming platform with a recurring monthly fee, users can purchase and hold a specific utility token that grants them access. This token can be spent incrementally or exchanged if the user discontinues the service, providing liquidity and value retention.

The use of utility tokens in tokenized services extends beyond consumer applications. Businesses are leveraging tokens to streamline operations and create more dynamic ecosystems. In cloud computing, for instance, companies introduce tokens allowing users to purchase storage or computing power on a decentralized network. This model eliminates the need for centralized intermediaries and fosters competition among service providers, driving down costs and improving efficiency.

Decentralized learning platforms are also utilizing utility tokens to create new educational paradigms. By tokenizing access to courses, certifications, and tutoring services, these platforms empower learners to invest in their education while retaining control over their digital assets. Tokens earned through participation or contributions can unlock additional resources, incentivizing engagement and creating a self-sustaining ecosystem.

The success of tokenized services relies heavily on community-driven growth, a hallmark of decentralized networks and utility tokens. In traditional systems, growth is often top-down, driven by centralized organizations with limited user input. Utility tokens invert this model, placing the community at the center of development and decision-making processes. This participatory approach fosters engagement, loyalty, and innovation, ensuring that platforms evolve in line with the needs and priorities of their users.

Community-driven growth is particularly evident in decentralized governance models, where token holders are empowered to propose and vote on changes to the platform. This level of involvement creates a sense of ownership and accountability, motivating users to actively contribute to the ecosystem. In addition to governance, communities play a vital role in promoting and expanding the reach of utility token platforms. Grassroots efforts, social media campaigns, and peer-to-peer interactions drive awareness and adoption, amplifying the impact of utility tokens.

Incentive mechanisms built into utility token platforms further fuel community growth. By rewarding users for participation, such as providing liquidity, creating content, or completing tasks, these platforms create a virtuous cycle of engagement and value creation. The rewards, often distributed as additional tokens, encourage users to remain active and invested in the ecosystem. Over time, this community-driven momentum can propel platforms to new heights, attracting developers, investors, and partners.

Utility tokens' ability to foster community-driven growth extends to addressing global challenges. Decentralized platforms supported by utility tokens are used to mobilize resources for social impact initiatives, from funding renewable energy projects to supporting disaster relief efforts. These projects leverage the power of communities to drive meaningful change, highlighting the potential of utility tokens to create a more inclusive and equitable digital economy.

Partnerships with enterprises represent another

significant opportunity for utility tokens, bridging the gap between decentralized innovation and traditional business practices. While blockchain technology has often been viewed as disruptive, many enterprises recognize its potential to complement and enhance their operations. Utility tokens are pivotal in this integration, enabling enterprises to tap into decentralized networks and unlock new revenue streams, efficiencies, and market opportunities.

One area where enterprise partnerships are thriving is in supply chain management. By integrating utility tokens into their operations, companies can tokenize assets, such as raw materials or finished goods, and track them across the supply chain. This tokenization enhances transparency, reduces fraud, and streamlines processes, creating a more resilient and efficient system. Additionally, utility tokens can incentivize stakeholders, such as suppliers and logistics providers, to adhere to best practices and meet sustainability goals.

The financial sector is also exploring the potential of utility tokens through partnerships with blockchain platforms. Banks and financial institutions leverage tokens to tokenize traditional assets, such as stocks, bonds, and real estate, creating fractionalized ownership and increasing liquidity. Utility tokens enable these institutions to offer innovative products and services, such as tokenized ETFs or decentralized lending platforms, attracting new investors and borrowers.

In digital identity, enterprises are partnering with blockchain platforms to develop solutions that empower users to own and control their personal data. Utility tokens facilitate the secure exchange of information, ensuring users can verify their identity without revealing sensitive details. These partnerships are particularly valuable in industries like healthcare, where privacy and security are paramount.

Utility tokens in enterprise partnerships can foster innovation and collaboration. By integrating tokens into their ecosystems, enterprises can incentivize developers to create apps, tools, and services that enhance their platforms. This open innovation model accelerates development and expands the utility of tokens, driving growth for both the enterprise and the blockchain ecosystem.

Emerging opportunities in utility tokens are reshaping how we interact with technology, communities, and businesses. Tokenized services are revolutionizing access to digital platforms, creating more flexible and efficient models for consuming and delivering value. Community-driven growth empowers users to take ownership of decentralized networks, fostering engagement and innovation. Partnerships with enterprises are bridging the divide between decentralized and traditional systems, unlocking new possibilities for collaboration and transformation.

As utility tokens continue to evolve, their impact will extend far beyond the cryptocurrency space, influencing industries and shaping the future of the digital economy. By embracing these emerging opportunities, developers, users, and businesses can harness the full potential of utility tokens, driving innovation and creating value in previously unimaginable ways. The future of utility tokens is not just about technology but about reimagining how we connect, collaborate, and create in a decentralized world.

# CHAPTER 7: GREEN ALTCOINS AND SUSTAINABILITY

*"Sustainable investing is about doing good and doing well."* — Larry Fink

Fink's statement aligns perfectly with green altcoins' mission, which combines environmental responsibility with technological innovation. As concerns over blockchain's energy consumption grow, these altcoins are stepping forward with solutions prioritizing sustainability. Green altcoins demonstrate that technological advancement and ecological stewardship can coexist by adopting energy-efficient consensus mechanisms like proof-of-stake or creating carbon-negative networks.

Algorand, for instance, has committed to a carbon-negative blockchain, offsetting its environmental impact through partnerships and renewable energy initiatives. Similarly, projects like Nano and SolarCoin focus on minimal energy consumption while maintaining high transaction efficiency. These altcoins address the environmental criticisms often directed at proof-of-work systems, offering viable alternatives that appeal to eco-conscious investors and developers.

The rise of green altcoins reflects a broader shift toward sustainability in the financial and technological sectors. Investors increasingly seek projects that align with their values, making environmentally friendly altcoins more attractive. These projects mitigate ecological impact and set new standards for the blockchain industry, encouraging other networks to adopt sustainable practices.

Fink's insight highlights the dual benefit of green altcoins: they generate financial returns while contributing to a more sustainable future. As the demand for eco-friendly solutions grows, green altcoins are poised to lead in shaping blockchain technology's evolution and its relationship with the environment.

The cryptocurrency industry, celebrated for its innovation and potential to decentralize economies, has faced significant criticism regarding its environmental impact. The energy consumption of blockchain networks, particularly those employing proof-of-work (PoW) consensus mechanisms, has become contentious. As concerns about climate change and sustainability intensify globally, the crypto sector has responded by exploring greener solutions, resulting in the emergence of green altcoins and a shift toward energy-efficient technologies. Understanding the environmental debate in crypto, the criticisms of high energy use, the shift toward sustainable solutions, and the comparison between proof-of-work and proof-of-stake (PoS) systems highlight the transformative potential of blockchain technology in aligning with sustainability goals.

The environmental debate in cryptocurrency gained prominence as blockchain networks like Bitcoin and Ethereum rose in popularity. PoW networks rely on mining, a process where computers solve complex mathematical problems to validate transactions and secure the blockchain. While secure and decentralized, this process is energy-intensive and requires substantial computational power. The energy consumption of Bitcoin, for example, has been compared to that of entire countries, drawing criticism from environmentalists, regulators, and industry observers. As cryptocurrencies gained mainstream attention, their ecological footprint became a focal point of discussions about their long-term viability and ethical implications.

Critics argue that the high energy consumption of PoW networks undermines the benefits of blockchain technology, particularly in an era of growing environmental awareness. The reliance on fossil fuels to power mining operations has raised concerns about greenhouse gas emissions, exacerbating global warming and climate change. Additionally, mining is often concentrated in regions with access to cheap but non-renewable energy sources, further compounding the environmental impact. For instance, some mining operations have relied on coal-fired power plants, creating significant carbon footprints and sparking public backlash.

Cryptocurrency's environmental criticism has also highlighted disparities in resource allocation. Large-scale mining operations, often backed by institutional investors, dominate the industry, leaving smaller participants with limited access to rewards. This concentration of power undermines the decentralized ethos of blockchain technology and raises questions about the crypto economy's social and environmental equity. Critics argue that the energy and resources consumed by mining could be better allocated to more pressing societal needs, such as renewable energy development or climate mitigation efforts.

In response to these criticisms, the crypto industry has begun a shift toward sustainable solutions, giving rise to a new wave of green altcoins and energy-efficient technologies. These initiatives reflect a growing recognition that the future of cryptocurrency must align with global sustainability goals to remain viable and ethical. Green altcoins are designed to minimize energy consumption and reduce environmental impact, employing innovative technologies and consensus mechanisms that prioritize efficiency and sustainability.

One of the most significant trends in this shift is the adoption of proof-of-stake (PoS) consensus mechanisms. Unlike PoW, which relies on energy-intensive mining, PoS achieves consensus by allowing participants to validate transactions based on the number of tokens they hold and are willing to stake as collateral. This approach eliminates the need for resource-intensive computations, drastically reducing energy consumption while maintaining the security and decentralization of the network. PoS has become a popular choice for new blockchain projects and is being adopted by existing networks, including Ethereum, which transitioned to PoS in a significant upgrade known as "The Merge."

The transition to PoS has sparked interest in green altcoins that already employ sustainable consensus mechanisms. These altcoins not only address environmental concerns but also demonstrate the potential of blockchain technology to support innovative and energy-efficient applications. For instance, projects like Algorand and Cardano have positioned themselves as leaders in the green crypto space by emphasizing sustainability in their design and operations. These platforms leverage PoS to achieve scalability, security, and low energy usage, making them attractive to environmentally conscious developers and investors.

Beyond consensus mechanisms, green altcoins are exploring other strategies to enhance sustainability. Some projects are integrating carbon offsetting initiatives, where a portion of transaction fees or token rewards is allocated to environmental programs, such as reforestation or renewable energy development. Others are partnering with sustainable energy providers to ensure their networks are powered by clean and renewable sources. These efforts highlight the industry's potential to minimize environmental impact and contribute positively to global sustainability goals.

Comparing proof-of-work and proof-of-stake systems reveals the stark differences in their environmental footprints and operational characteristics. PoW, the original consensus mechanism used by Bitcoin and other early cryptocurrencies, is renowned for its security and decentralization. PoW makes it economically and logistically challenging for bad actors to compromise the network by requiring miners to expend computational power and energy. However, this security comes at a high environmental cost, as mining operations consume vast electricity and produce significant carbon emissions.

PoS, on the other hand, achieves similar levels of security and decentralization through economic incentives rather than computational power. Validators in a PoS system are selected based on the number of tokens they hold and are willing to lock as collateral. This approach eliminates the need for energy-intensive mining, reducing electricity consumption by up to 99% compared to PoW. Additionally, PoS networks can achieve faster transaction speeds and greater scalability, making them more suitable for a wide range of applications beyond cryptocurrency.

While PoS offers significant environmental advantages, it also has its critics. Some argue that PoS networks may favor wealthier participants who can afford to stake more tokens, potentially leading to centralization. Others raise concerns about the complexity of PoS implementations and the potential for new vulnerabilities. Despite these challenges, the rapid adoption of PoS reflects a growing consensus that energy efficiency is critical for the future of blockchain technology.

The transition from PoW to PoS and the emergence of green altcoins signal a broader shift in the crypto industry toward sustainability. This evolution is not just about addressing environmental concerns; it is about redefining the role of blockchain technology in a world that prioritizes resilience, equity, and ethical innovation. By embracing sustainable solutions, the crypto sector can demonstrate its commitment to being a positive force for change, inspiring confidence among users, regulators, and investors.

The environmental debate in crypto has highlighted the need for innovation and accountability in the pursuit of decentralized technologies. While criticisms of high energy use are valid, the industry's response through green altcoins and sustainable practices demonstrates its capacity for self-correction and growth. By prioritizing energy efficiency and aligning with global sustainability goals, blockchain technology can fulfill its potential as a transformative force for good, enabling economic inclusion, technological progress, and environmental stewardship in the digital age.

## Leading The Green Crypto Movement

As the cryptocurrency industry grapples with criticism over its environmental impact, a new wave of projects has emerged to address these concerns and redefine blockchain technology's relationship with sustainability. The green crypto movement represents a commitment to minimizing energy consumption, reducing carbon footprints, and aligning blockchain innovation with global environmental goals. Among the leaders of this movement are SolarCoin, Nano, and Algorand. These projects have distinguished themselves through unique approaches emphasizing energy efficiency, incentivizing clean energy production, and prioritizing carbon-negative initiatives.

SolarCoin stands out as a pioneer in incentivizing the generation of clean energy. Designed as a digital reward for solar energy producers, SolarCoin's mission is to accelerate the transition to renewable energy by creating an additional financial incentive for individuals and organizations to adopt solar technology. Unlike traditional cryptocurrencies that rely on energy-intensive mining, SolarCoin operates on a lightweight blockchain designed for efficiency. Each SolarCoin represents one megawatt-hour (MWh) of solar energy generated, and recipients can claim these tokens as a reward for their contributions to clean energy production.

The impact of SolarCoin extends beyond the cryptocurrency space, as it directly supports the global shift toward renewable energy. By providing an additional income stream for solar energy producers, SolarCoin reduces the payback period for solar installations, making the technology more accessible and appealing. This model empowers individual producers and supports large-scale solar farms and corporate sustainability initiatives. By connecting the financial incentives of blockchain technology with the environmental benefits of solar energy, SolarCoin bridges the gap between digital innovation and tangible climate action.

SolarCoin's potential as a green crypto leader is amplified by its scalability and global reach. The platform is designed to accommodate a growing number of solar energy producers, from small residential systems to utility-scale projects. Its decentralized nature ensures transparency and trust, as all transactions are recorded on the blockchain, creating a verifiable record of solar energy production. This transparency enhances SolarCoin's credibility as a tool for incentivizing and tracking renewable energy adoption.

While SolarCoin focuses on directly supporting renewable energy, Nano emphasizes energy efficiency in its design and operation. Nano was created to address one of the most significant criticisms of traditional cryptocurrencies: the high energy consumption associated with mining and transaction processing. Unlike proof-of-work (PoW) systems requiring substantial computational power, Nano employs a novel consensus mechanism called Open Representative Voting (ORV). This approach eliminates the need for mining entirely, enabling near-instant transactions with minimal energy use.

Nano's energy efficiency is environmentally friendly and enhances its utility as a digital currency. Transactions on the Nano network are processed quickly and without fees, making it an ideal solution for everyday payments and microtransactions. This combination of speed, affordability, and sustainability positions Nano as a viable alternative to traditional cryptocurrencies and conventional payment systems. By prioritizing energy efficiency, Nano demonstrates that blockchain technology can deliver high performance without compromising environmental values.

The environmental advantages of Nano extend beyond its low energy consumption. The simplicity of its design reduces the infrastructure required to operate the network, minimizing its overall ecological impact. Nano's lightweight protocol ensures that even low-power devices, such as smartphones and IoT devices, can participate in the network, expanding accessibility and reducing the digital divide. This inclusivity aligns with the broader goals of the green crypto movement, which seeks to make blockchain technology both sustainable and universally accessible.

Algorand takes sustainability a step further by incorporating carbon-negative initiatives into its operations. Built on a proof-of-stake (PoS) consensus mechanism, Algorand is designed to be energy-efficient from the ground up. The network's PoS model eliminates the need for energy-intensive mining, significantly reducing its carbon footprint. However, Algorand's commitment to sustainability goes beyond energy efficiency. The platform has partnered with environmental organizations to offset its carbon emissions, ensuring its operations are carbon-neutral and carbon-negative.

Algorand's approach to sustainability is integrated into its governance and ecosystem development.

The platform allocates some transaction fees and block rewards to fund carbon offset projects, such as reforestation and renewable energy initiatives. These efforts demonstrate Algorand's commitment to using blockchain technology as a force for positive environmental change. By aligning its economic incentives with sustainability goals, Algorand sets a standard for the industry, showing that environmental responsibility can coexist with innovation and growth.

The impact of Algorand's carbon-negative initiatives extends beyond its network, inspiring other blockchain projects to adopt similar practices. Algorand encourages the broader crypto community to prioritize sustainability by demonstrating the feasibility and benefits of carbon offsets. Its leadership in this area has earned recognition from environmental advocates and industry stakeholders, positioning Algorand as a model for integrating ecological stewardship into blockchain development.

The efforts of SolarCoin, Nano, and Algorand highlight the diversity of approaches within the green crypto movement. Each project addresses different aspects of sustainability, from incentivizing renewable energy production to optimizing energy efficiency and implementing carbon-negative practices. Together, they represent a holistic vision for the future of cryptocurrency, where innovation and environmental responsibility go hand in hand.

The success of these green altcoins also underscores the potential for blockchain technology to contribute to broader sustainability goals. Addressing the environmental criticisms of traditional cryptocurrencies, these projects demonstrate that blockchain can be a powerful tool for advancing climate action, promoting renewable energy, and reducing global carbon emissions. As the crypto industry continues to evolve, the green crypto movement offers a blueprint for aligning technological progress with the urgent need for sustainability.

SolarCoin, Nano, and Algorand are more than just leading examples of green cryptocurrencies; they are catalysts for change in the blockchain industry. Their commitment to sustainability and innovative use of blockchain technology pave the way for a future where digital currencies and decentralized systems play a central role in creating a more sustainable world. By embracing the principles of the green crypto movement, these projects not only address the challenges of today but also set the stage for a more equitable and environmentally conscious future.

**Future of Sustainability in Altcoins**
The future of altcoins is increasingly tied to their ability to address sustainability challenges and meet the growing demands of investors, communities, and governments. The push for green technologies and eco-friendly blockchain solutions has become a defining trend as environmental concerns intersect with the rapid expansion of decentralized finance and digital assets. Altcoins prioritizing sustainability are uniquely positioned to lead this shift, aligning technological innovation with global goals for reducing carbon footprints and fostering environmental resilience.

Investor and community demands for sustainable practices are reshaping the cryptocurrency landscape.

As environmental, social, and governance (ESG) considerations gain prominence in financial markets, investors are increasingly scrutinizing the environmental impact of their portfolios. Cryptocurrencies, particularly those relying on energy-intensive proof-of-work (PoW) mechanisms, have come under fire for their significant carbon emissions. This scrutiny has led to a shift in investment strategies, with institutional and retail investors favoring projects demonstrating a sustainability commitment.

Altcoins that align with ESG principles are finding themselves at an advantage in this evolving landscape. Investors are drawn to projects incorporating energy-efficient consensus mechanisms, carbon offset initiatives, and partnerships with renewable energy providers. These features mitigate environmental impact and enhance the marketability and long-term viability of altcoins. Sustainability-focused projects appeal to a growing demographic of environmentally conscious investors who seek to balance financial returns with ethical considerations.

Community engagement is another critical factor driving the demand for sustainable altcoins. The decentralized nature of blockchain technology empowers communities to influence the direction and priorities of projects. In many cases, token holders participate in governance decisions, using their voting power to advocate for environmental initiatives and sustainable practices. This participatory model ensures that sustainability is not just a marketing strategy but a core value embedded in the decision-making processes of blockchain ecosystems.

Communities also play a vital role in promoting and adopting green technologies. Grassroots campaigns, social media advocacy, and educational efforts amplify the visibility of sustainability-focused altcoins, encouraging wider adoption and support. This organic growth, fueled by engaged and motivated communities, strengthens the market position of eco-friendly projects and inspires other blockchain platforms to prioritize environmental responsibility.

The government's push for green technologies further accelerates the transition to sustainable altcoins. As nations confront the challenges of climate change and carbon emissions, policymakers are increasingly recognizing the need to regulate and incentivize environmentally friendly practices within the cryptocurrency sector. This recognition has resulted in a mix of regulatory pressures and supportive measures to steer the industry toward sustainability.

Some governments have introduced regulations targeting energy-intensive mining operations, requiring them to transition to renewable energy sources or face penalties. Others actively support the development of green blockchain technologies through grants, subsidies, and public-private partnerships. These initiatives create a favorable environment for altcoins that prioritize sustainability, encouraging innovation and investment in eco-friendly solutions.

The alignment of blockchain technology with government goals for green energy transition is particularly significant. Altcoins integrating renewable energy into their operations or directly supporting clean energy initiatives, such as SolarCoin, exemplify how cryptocurrencies can contribute to national and global sustainability agendas. By demonstrating their potential to reduce emissions, improve energy efficiency, and drive technological progress, these projects gain credibility and support from policymakers.

Scaling eco-friendly blockchain solutions is critical for ensuring that sustainability-focused altcoins can meet the demands of growing adoption and expanding ecosystems. While many altcoins have successfully reduced their environmental impact through innovative consensus mechanisms, such as proof-of-stake (PoS), scalability remains challenging. As more users and applications join blockchain networks, the need for efficient, low-energy solutions becomes increasingly urgent.

Layer-2 scaling solutions, which process transactions off the main blockchain to reduce congestion and energy consumption, are emerging as a key strategy for addressing scalability challenges. These solutions enable altcoins to maintain high performance while minimizing their environmental footprint. Blockchain networks can process transactions more efficiently by leveraging technologies like rollups, sidechains, and state channels, reducing energy use and transaction costs.

Interoperability is another critical aspect of scaling eco-friendly blockchain solutions. By enabling seamless interactions between different blockchains, interoperability reduces resource duplication and enhances the overall efficiency of decentralized systems. Altcoins that prioritize interoperability not only expand their utility but also contribute to the sustainability of the broader blockchain ecosystem. This interconnectedness fosters collaboration and innovation, allowing networks to share resources and best practices for minimizing environmental impact.

Advancements in cryptographic techniques also hold promise for scaling eco-friendly altcoins. Technologies like zero-knowledge proofs and zk-STARKs enable efficient and secure transaction verification, reducing the computational requirements of blockchain networks. These innovations enhance the scalability and sustainability of altcoins, ensuring that they can accommodate growing demand without compromising environmental values.

The role of renewable energy in scaling eco-friendly blockchain solutions cannot be overstated. Many altcoins are exploring partnerships with renewable energy providers to power their operations and reduce their reliance on fossil fuels. By integrating clean energy sources, these projects lower their carbon footprints and align with global efforts to transition to sustainable energy systems. Renewable energy adoption also enhances the resilience and independence of blockchain networks, reducing their vulnerability to fluctuations in energy markets.

The future of sustainability in altcoins is a convergence of technological innovation, community advocacy, and regulatory support. As investor and community demands for eco-friendly practices grow, altcoins prioritizing sustainability are gaining a competitive edge that appeals to many stakeholders. Governments are pivotal in driving this transition, creating an environment that encourages the adoption of green technologies and supports the development of energy-efficient blockchain solutions.

Scaling these solutions is essential for ensuring sustainability remains a central focus as blockchain technology evolves and expands. By leveraging advancements in scaling techniques, interoperability, cryptographic innovations, and renewable energy integration, altcoins can address the challenges of adoption and growth while maintaining their commitment to environmental responsibility.

The future of sustainability in altcoins represents an opportunity to redefine the cryptocurrency industry's relationship with the environment. By embracing sustainable practices, altcoins can demonstrate their capacity for positive impact, building trust and credibility among users, investors, and regulators. This alignment of technology and sustainability addresses past criticisms and paves the way for a future where blockchain innovation supports a greener, more equitable world. As the green crypto movement continues to gain momentum, altcoins can potentially lead the charge in transforming the digital economy into a force for environmental resilience and progress.

# CHAPTER 8: INSTITUTIONAL ADOPTION OF ALTCOINS

*"Institutional adoption of crypto assets is just beginning."* — Michael Sonnenshein.

Sonnenshein's observation reflects a pivotal moment in the cryptocurrency market as institutions embrace altcoins as part of their portfolios and operations. This shift brings credibility, stability, and significant capital to the altcoin ecosystem, signaling a move toward mainstream acceptance. Institutions such as Tesla, MicroStrategy, and PayPal have already made headlines with their adoption of cryptocurrencies, demonstrating the growing confidence in blockchain-based assets.

Institutional interest in altcoins extends beyond Bitcoin and Ethereum. Altcoins like Solana, Cardano, and Polkadot are attracting attention for their advanced scalability, speed, and interoperability capabilities. These features align with the needs of enterprise applications, making altcoins valuable tools for innovation in finance, supply chain management, and data security.

The involvement of institutional investors also fosters market maturity. Their participation introduces higher levels of scrutiny, due diligence, and regulatory compliance, which benefit the broader ecosystem. Additionally, institutions bring the financial infrastructure needed to support large-scale adoption, including custodial services, trading platforms, and research. Sonnenshein's insight underscores the transformative impact of institutional adoption on the altcoin market. As more institutions recognize the potential of altcoins, they will drive growth, innovation, and integration into traditional systems, solidifying the role of cryptocurrencies in the global economy.

◆ ◆ ◆

Institutions' growing adoption of altcoins marks a significant turning point in the cryptocurrency landscape, shifting its perception from speculative assets to integral components of corporate strategies. With their diverse functionalities and applications, businesses increasingly leverage Altcoins to streamline operations, enhance transparency, and revolutionize financial and operational systems. Their role in corporate use cases, particularly in streamlining supply chains, revolutionizing payments, and bolstering data security and transparency, underscores the transformative potential of altcoins in institutional contexts, inspiring a new wave of innovation and efficiency.

Altcoins tailored for corporate use cases reshape how businesses operate in an increasingly digital and interconnected world. Enterprises recognize the value of blockchain technology and altcoins in addressing inefficiencies, reducing costs, and enhancing the security of critical processes. Unlike traditional cryptocurrencies such as Bitcoin, which primarily serve as a store of value, altcoins are often designed with specific functionalities that align with corporate needs. These functionalities include tokenized incentives, access to decentralized networks, and integration with advanced technologies such as smart contracts and Internet of Things (IoT) devices.

One of the most impactful applications of altcoins in corporate settings is their role in streamlining supply chains. The global nature of modern supply chains and their complexity and fragmentation have long presented challenges for businesses. Traditional systems often rely on manual processes, multiple intermediaries, and siloed data, leading to inefficiencies, increased costs, and limited transparency. Altcoins and blockchain technology address these issues by providing a decentralized, transparent, and immutable record of transactions and activities across the supply chain.

By tokenizing assets and processes, altcoins enable real-time tracking and verifying goods as they move through the supply chain. For instance, products can be tagged with blockchain-encoded identifiers that record their origin, manufacturing details, transportation milestones, and storage conditions. This information, stored on a decentralized ledger, is accessible to all authorized participants, ensuring transparency and accountability at every stage. Altcoins facilitate these interactions by serving as the medium of exchange or incentivizing compliance with agreed-upon standards.

The benefits of altcoin integration in supply chains extend beyond operational efficiencies. Transparency enabled by blockchain technology enhances trust among stakeholders, including suppliers, manufacturers, distributors, and consumers. For industries such as food and pharmaceuticals, where traceability and authenticity are critical, altcoins provide a reliable mechanism for verifying the provenance and quality of products. This capability is particularly valuable in addressing issues such as counterfeit goods, fraud, and ethical sourcing, as it empowers consumers and regulators with verifiable data.

Enterprises are also leveraging altcoins to revolutionize payments, creating faster, cheaper, and more secure transaction systems. Traditional payment methods, particularly in cross-border contexts, often involve high fees, lengthy processing times, and multiple intermediaries. Altcoins offer a solution by enabling direct, peer-to-peer transactions on decentralized networks, bypassing the need for intermediaries and reducing transaction costs. This practical application of altcoins in revolutionizing payments underscores their potential to bring tangible benefits to businesses.

Altcoins such as XRP, Stellar (XLM), and stablecoins like USDC are specifically designed to facilitate efficient payments. XRP, for example, is used by financial institutions to enable real-time, low-cost cross-border payments. Its integration into RippleNet, a blockchain-based payment network, has transformed how banks and payment providers settle international transactions. By eliminating the need for pre-funded accounts and intermediaries, XRP reduces liquidity costs and accelerates settlement times, benefiting both businesses and consumers.

Stablecoins have emerged as another powerful tool for revolutionizing payments in corporate contexts. Pegged to stable assets like fiat currencies or commodities, stablecoins mitigate the volatility associated with traditional cryptocurrencies, making them ideal for commercial transactions. Businesses can use stablecoins to pay suppliers, manage payroll, and settle international invoices without the delays and fees associated with traditional banking systems. Additionally, stablecoins enable programmable money, where smart contracts automate payment processes based on predefined conditions, further enhancing efficiency and accuracy.

Adopting altcoins in payments is not limited to financial institutions and large corporations. Small and medium-sized enterprises (SMEs) are also exploring the benefits of integrating altcoins into their payment systems. By accepting altcoins as a form of payment, SMEs can tap into new customer bases, particularly among tech-savvy and cryptocurrency-enthusiast demographics. Altcoins also enable SMEs to participate in decentralized marketplaces, where they can transact directly with customers and suppliers, reducing reliance on third-party platforms.

Data security and transparency represent another critical area where altcoins drive institutional adoption. In an era where data breaches and cyberattacks are increasingly common, businesses face growing pressure to secure sensitive information while ensuring compliance with privacy and regulatory standards. With its decentralized and tamper-proof design, blockchain technology offers a robust solution for enhancing data security and transparency. Altcoins are the foundation for these systems, facilitating secure access, data sharing, and recordkeeping. This underscores their role in addressing critical business needs.

Integrating altcoins into data management systems enables businesses to create decentralized identities and data-sharing frameworks. Decentralized identities empower individuals and organizations to own and control their data, granting access only to authorized parties. Altcoins are used to authenticate and manage these interactions, ensuring that sensitive information remains secure and private. For example, in healthcare, decentralized identity systems powered by altcoins allow patients to share medical records with providers securely, reducing the risk of data breaches and ensuring compliance with regulations like HIPAA.

Transparency enabled by blockchain technology is

equally transformative for industries that require verifiable and auditable records. In finance, for example, altcoins are being used to power platforms that provide real-time transparency into transactions, audits, and regulatory compliance. These platforms eliminate the need for manual reconciliation and enhance trust between stakeholders. Similarly, in supply chains, blockchain-based records ensure that production, transportation, and distribution data is accurate, immutable, and accessible to authorized participants.

The potential of altcoins to enhance data security and transparency is particularly significant in public sector applications. Governments and regulatory bodies are exploring blockchain technology to improve the efficiency and integrity of public services, such as voting systems, land registries, and tax collection. Altcoins facilitate these initiatives by enabling secure transactions, incentivizing participation, and providing a transparent record of activities. For instance, in voting systems, blockchain technology powered by altcoins can ensure that ballots are immutable and verifiable, enhancing trust in the democratic process.

The institutional adoption of altcoins represents a paradigm shift in how businesses and organizations leverage blockchain technology to address operational challenges and unlock new opportunities. From streamlining supply chains and revolutionizing payments to enhancing data security and transparency, altcoins are redefining the role of digital assets in corporate and public sector contexts. Their ability to deliver tangible benefits, such as significant cost savings, efficiency gains, and trust-building, underscores their growing relevance in a rapidly digitalizing world, instilling a sense of optimism about the financial benefits of altcoin integration.

As altcoins continue to gain traction among institutions, their adoption will drive further innovation and integration, paving the way for more advanced use cases and applications. The future of altcoins lies not only in their technical capabilities but also in their ability to adapt to the evolving needs of businesses, governments, and communities. By addressing real-world challenges and delivering measurable value, altcoins are poised to become an indispensable tool for institutions seeking to thrive in an increasingly decentralized and interconnected global economy.

## Trends In Institutional Investments

Institutional investments in cryptocurrencies have grown exponentially over the past decade, signaling a significant shift in how traditional financial entities perceive the digital asset market. While Bitcoin and Ethereum initially dominated institutional interest, a growing trend toward diversification through altcoins has emerged. This evolution highlights the willingness of institutional investors to explore new opportunities within the cryptocurrency ecosystem. Early adopters of crypto funds paved the way for this shift, and real-world case studies of altcoin adoption by institutions underscore their potential for transforming investment strategies.

Early adopters of crypto funds played a critical role in legitimizing cryptocurrencies as an asset class for institutional portfolios. These pioneering investors recognized the disruptive potential of blockchain technology and saw value in gaining exposure to the nascent cryptocurrency market. Hedge funds, venture capital firms, and even publicly traded companies were among the first to allocate capital to digital assets, challenging the traditional notions of risk and diversification.

One of the earliest examples of institutional adoption was the establishment of crypto-focused hedge funds. Firms such as Pantera Capital and Polychain Capital emerged in the early 2010s, specializing in investments across the cryptocurrency spectrum. These funds identified opportunities in Bitcoin and Ethereum while investing in emerging altcoins and blockchain projects. Their success demonstrated that cryptocurrencies could deliver outsized returns compared to traditional asset classes, attracting attention from other institutional players.

Publicly traded companies, such as MicroStrategy, also played a key role in shaping institutional interest in cryptocurrencies. In 2020, MicroStrategy made headlines by adopting Bitcoin as its primary treasury reserve asset. The move was driven by the company's belief that Bitcoin offered a superior store of value compared to fiat currencies. This bold decision boosted MicroStrategy's market profile and inspired other corporations to explore cryptocurrency investments. Over time, interest expanded from Bitcoin to altcoins as companies sought diversification and exposure to innovative blockchain ecosystems.

As the cryptocurrency market matured, institutional investors began recognizing the potential of altcoins to diversify portfolios and enhance returns. While Bitcoin and Ethereum remained foundational assets, altcoins offered unique value propositions that addressed specific use cases, industries, and technological challenges. This diversification allowed institutions to balance risk and reward while exploring new avenues for growth.

One reason altcoins became attractive to institutional investors was their ability to capture niche markets and drive innovation. Unlike Bitcoin, which primarily stores value, many altcoins are designed for specific applications. For example, Chainlink focuses on decentralized oracles, Filecoin targets decentralized storage, and Polkadot facilitates interoperability between blockchains. By investing in these altcoins, institutions could gain exposure to emerging technologies and industries poised for disruption.

The decentralized finance (DeFi) sector became a focal point for institutional altcoin investments. Platforms such as Uniswap, Aave, and Curve Finance, powered by their respective altcoins, demonstrated the potential of blockchain technology to revolutionize financial services. Institutional investors recognized the growth opportunities within DeFi and began allocating capital to tokens that supported these platforms. This interest drove the development of DeFi infrastructure and solidified the role of altcoins in the broader cryptocurrency ecosystem.

Another factor driving diversification through altcoins was the growing recognition of their role in environmental, social, and governance (ESG) strategies. As sustainability became a priority for investors, altcoins with energy-efficient consensus mechanisms, such as proof-of-stake (PoS), gained favor. Institutions seeking to align their portfolios with ESG principles began favoring altcoins like Algorand, Cardano, and Solana, demonstrating a commitment to reducing environmental impact.

The institutional adoption of altcoins has been further validated by real-world case studies highlighting their practical applications and financial potential. One notable example is the investment by Andreessen Horowitz (a16z), a prominent venture capital firm, in blockchain projects and altcoins. The firm's cryptocurrency-focused fund, a16z Crypto, has invested in a diverse portfolio of blockchain initiatives, from decentralized finance and gaming to infrastructure and Web3 platforms. This strategy underscores the potential of altcoins to deliver returns while supporting the growth of transformative technologies.

In another case, the Canadian investment firm Purpose Investments launched the world's first regulated Bitcoin ETF in 2021, followed shortly by an Ethereum ETF. This groundbreaking move opened the door for similar products focused on altcoins. The firm recognized that providing institutional-grade exposure to altcoins could attract investors seeking diversification and innovation. By integrating altcoins into their offerings, Purpose Investments helped bridge the gap between traditional finance and the cryptocurrency market.

The adoption of altcoins for tokenized real estate represents another compelling case study. Institutions and investment firms use blockchain technology and altcoins to fractionalize real estate assets, making them accessible to a broader range of investors. For example, platforms like RealT tokenize properties and enable investors to purchase fractional ownership using stablecoins or altcoins. This approach democratizes access to real estate, enhances liquidity, and streamlines the investment process, illustrating the versatility of altcoins in transforming traditional asset classes.

The rise of institutional interest in non-fungible tokens (NFTs) has also brought altcoins into the spotlight. NFTs, powered by altcoin-based platforms like Ethereum, Flow, and Tezos, have gained traction in the art, entertainment, and gaming industries. Institutions, including auction houses and media companies, have begun integrating NFTs into their strategies, leveraging the unique capabilities of altcoin ecosystems to create new revenue streams and engage audiences. These real-world applications demonstrate how altcoins can enable innovative business models and redefine traditional industries.

The development of infrastructure and services tailored to the needs of large-scale investors has facilitated the integration of altcoins into institutional portfolios. Custodial solutions, regulatory compliance frameworks, and risk management tools have all contributed to making altcoins more accessible and appealing to institutions. Platforms such as Coinbase Custody and Anchorage Digital provide secure storage for altcoins, ensuring that institutional investors can manage their holdings with confidence.

Regulatory clarity has also been crucial in encouraging institutional adoption of altcoins. While regulatory uncertainty remains a challenge in some jurisdictions, progress has been made in defining cryptocurrency investments' legal and compliance requirements. Institutions are now better equipped to navigate the regulatory landscape, enabling them to incorporate altcoins into their strategies while adhering to best practices and standards.

The trends in institutional investments highlight the transformative potential of altcoins as a key component of modern portfolios. Early adopters of crypto funds demonstrated the viability of digital assets, paving the way for broader acceptance and integration. Diversification through altcoins has allowed institutions to capture opportunities in niche markets, innovative technologies, and emerging industries. Real-world case studies of altcoin adoption further validate their value, illustrating how they can address practical challenges and deliver financial returns.

As the cryptocurrency market evolves, institutional investments in altcoins will likely expand further. The growing demand for diversification, innovation, and sustainability positions altcoins as a critical asset class for the future. By aligning their strategies with the unique capabilities of altcoins, institutions can navigate the complexities of a digital-first economy and capitalize on the opportunities blockchain technology presents. This shift represents a financial revolution and a broader transformation in how value is created, shared, and sustained in a decentralized world.

## Institutional Impact On Altcoin Markets

The growing participation of institutional investors in altcoin markets has had a profound impact on the cryptocurrency ecosystem. Institutions bring significant capital, expertise, and market credibility, which influence the dynamics of altcoin trading and adoption. Their involvement boosts credibility and stability, highlights the long-term market potential of altcoins, and introduces risks such as centralization that must be carefully managed. Understanding the institutional impact on altcoin markets provides insight into the evolving role of cryptocurrencies in the global financial system.

Institutional investment has been instrumental in enhancing the credibility of altcoins. When established financial entities such as hedge funds, venture capital firms, and publicly traded companies allocate capital to altcoins, they lend legitimacy to an asset class often viewed as speculative and volatile. Institutional interest signals confidence in the underlying technology and its potential applications, reassuring retail investors and the broader market about the viability of altcoins.

The participation of institutional investors also contributes to market stability. Unlike retail traders, who may engage in short-term speculation, institutions adopt long-term investment strategies.

Their large-scale investments and measured trading practices reduce market volatility, providing a stabilizing effect on altcoin prices. For example, when a major institution announces its involvement in a specific altcoin, it often leads to sustained price increases driven by renewed market confidence, as opposed to the rapid peaks and troughs caused by retail speculation.

Institutional investments have also fostered the development of a robust market infrastructure for altcoins. Custodial solutions, over-the-counter (OTC) trading desks, and regulatory-compliant exchanges have been established to meet the needs of institutional clients. These services provide secure and efficient avenues for trading and storing altcoins, further enhancing market trust and accessibility. Institutions can manage risk more effectively with these infrastructures, encouraging greater participation and larger investments.

The long-term market potential of altcoins is another significant aspect of institutional impact. Institutions increasingly view altcoins as speculative assets and key components of emerging technologies and industries. Altcoins power decentralized finance (DeFi) platforms, enable blockchain-based gaming ecosystems and facilitate innovations in supply chain management, healthcare, and real estate. Institutional investment in these altcoins reflects a belief in the transformative potential of blockchain technology and its applications across various sectors.

The shift toward sustainability has further highlighted the long-term potential of altcoins. As environmental, social, and governance (ESG) considerations become central to investment strategies, institutions focus on altcoins that align with these principles. Projects such as Algorand, Cardano, and Solana, which prioritize energy efficiency and sustainability, have garnered significant attention from institutional investors. This trend underscores the role of altcoins in driving innovation while addressing global challenges such as climate change and resource management.

Institutional involvement also accelerates the mainstream adoption of altcoins by bridging the gap between traditional finance and the cryptocurrency ecosystem. Institutions enable altcoins to penetrate established markets and industries through partnerships and integrations. For example, financial institutions incorporating altcoins into payment systems or investment products make them accessible to a broader audience, fostering greater awareness and usage. This integration expands the reach of altcoins and positions them as viable alternatives to traditional financial instruments.

Despite these benefits, the institutional impact on altcoin markets has risks, particularly the risk of centralization. One of the defining features of blockchain technology is its decentralized nature, which ensures that no single entity has disproportionate control over the network. However, the concentration of altcoin holdings among a few large institutional investors can undermine this principle, introducing elements of centralization into decentralized ecosystems.

When institutions hold significant portions of an

altcoin's supply, they gain outsized influence over the network's governance and decision-making processes. This concentration of power can lead to decisions prioritizing institutional interests over those of the broader community. For example, institutions might push for changes that align with regulatory compliance or profitability, even if these changes compromise decentralization or user privacy. Such actions can erode trust within the community and create tensions between different stakeholder groups.

The risk of market manipulation also increases with institutional involvement. Large-scale investors can influence altcoin prices through coordinated buying or selling, creating artificial volatility or price stability. While these practices may not be widespread, the potential for manipulation highlights the need for transparent and ethical trading practices in institutional markets. Regulators and industry leaders must work together to establish guidelines that promote fair and equitable participation for all market participants.

Another challenge associated with institutional impact is the potential for reduced innovation. Blockchain technology's open and experimental nature has fostered rapid innovation and the development of diverse altcoin ecosystems. However, institutional involvement often focuses on risk management, compliance, and profitability, which can limit the willingness to experiment with novel or unconventional ideas. While these considerations are necessary for scaling and sustainability, they may stifle creativity and slow the pace of innovation in certain areas.

The institutional focus on a select few altcoins can also marginalize smaller or emerging projects. As institutions allocate capital to established altcoins with proven use cases, less attention and funding may be directed toward newer or riskier ventures. This trend can create a concentration of resources around a handful of projects, reducing diversity within the altcoin market. It also raises barriers for new entrants, who may struggle to compete with well-funded incumbents.

Despite these risks, the institutional impact on altcoin markets has been positive, driving growth, stability, and innovation. To address the challenges, a balanced approach that fosters collaboration between institutions and decentralized communities is needed. Transparent governance structures, inclusive decision-making processes, and ethical trading practices can help mitigate the risks of centralization and ensure that altcoin ecosystems remain open and equitable.

Regulators and industry bodies are also critical in shaping the institutional impact on altcoin markets. Clear and consistent regulatory frameworks give institutions the confidence to participate while protecting the interests of retail investors and smaller stakeholders. Collaboration between regulators, institutions, and blockchain projects can create a balanced ecosystem that supports growth and innovation without compromising the principles of decentralization.

The institutional impact on altcoin markets represents

a pivotal moment in the evolution of cryptocurrency. Institutions bring much-needed credibility, stability, and resources, enhancing the market's maturity and attractiveness. At the same time, their involvement introduces risks and challenges that must be carefully managed to preserve the core values of blockchain technology. By addressing these issues, the cryptocurrency ecosystem can harness the benefits of institutional participation while maintaining its commitment to decentralization, innovation, and inclusivity. The future of altcoins will be shaped by how effectively these dynamics are navigated, paving the way for a more integrated and resilient financial landscape.

# CHAPTER 9: EVALUATING ALTCOIN PROJECTS

*"Do your own research before making any investment decisions."* — Brian Armstrong

Armstrong's advice highlights the critical importance of due diligence in the altcoin market, where innovation and speculation often blur the lines between opportunity and risk. With thousands of altcoin projects vying for attention, understanding the fundamentals of each one is essential for making informed decisions. Successful investing in altcoins requires evaluating key factors such as the team behind the project, its real-world utility, adoption potential, and community support. Ambitious goals often drive altcoin projects, but not all are grounded in feasible strategies or sustainable models. Researching the development team's experience and credibility can provide insights into the project's potential for success. Additionally, analyzing the tokenomics, including supply mechanisms and incentive structures, helps investors determine the viability of an altcoin as a long-term investment.

Community engagement and developer activity are critical indicators of a project's health. Projects with active communities and strong developer ecosystems will likely thrive and adapt to challenges. Platforms like GitHub can provide valuable information about a project's technical progress and the commitment of its contributors.

Armstrong's statement reminds us that informed decisions are the foundation of successful altcoin investing. Investors can identify projects with genuine value and long-term potential by conducting thorough research and avoiding reliance on hype or speculation. In a rapidly evolving market, knowledge is the most powerful tool for mitigating risks and capitalizing on opportunities.

The explosive growth of the cryptocurrency market has created a dynamic and diverse landscape for altcoins, offering many promising opportunities. Investors, developers, and enthusiasts are continuously evaluating altcoin projects, navigating the complexities of the market with optimism and hope. Evaluating altcoins effectively is essential for making informed decisions and mitigating risks. Factors such as key metrics, market capitalization, developer activity, and token utility provide critical insights into the potential and sustainability of altcoin projects.

Key metrics form the foundation for evaluating the health and viability of an altcoin project. These metrics help investors and stakeholders assess a cryptocurrency's performance, growth, and stability. Analyzing metrics such as trading volume, volatility, and historical price trends provides a snapshot of an altcoin's market dynamics. High trading volumes often indicate strong interest and liquidity, which are essential for a vibrant market. Conversely, low trading volumes may signal limited adoption or waning interest, raising questions about an altcoin's long-term viability.

Volatility is another important metric that reflects an altcoin's price fluctuations over time. While cryptocurrencies are inherently volatile, excessive or unpredictable swings in price can deter institutional and retail investors, making it crucial to evaluate an altcoin's risk-reward profile. Assessing volatility alongside trading volume clarifies how resilient an altcoin is to market sentiment and external shocks. Historical price trends further complement this analysis by revealing patterns, peaks, and downturns that help predict future performance.

Market capitalization and circulating supply are among the most widely used metrics for evaluating altcoins. Market cap is calculated by multiplying an altcoin's current price by its circulating supply, offering a measure of the total value of a cryptocurrency in the market. Altcoins with high market caps are often perceived as stable and established, while those with lower market caps may present higher risks and greater growth potential. Understanding the relationship between market cap and an altcoin's market position helps investors determine its competitiveness within the broader cryptocurrency ecosystem.

Circulating supply provides insights into the availability of tokens in the market. An altcoin with a limited supply may experience upward price pressure as demand grows, making it attractive to investors seeking scarcity-driven value. On the other hand, projects with excessive token supplies may struggle to maintain price stability, especially if demand fails to keep pace with supply. It is also important to consider whether the circulating supply is fixed or inflationary, as inflationary models introduce new tokens over time, potentially diluting the value of existing holdings.

Developer activity serves as a vital indicator of an altcoin project's growth and sustainability. Active development signals a commitment to improving the project's technology, addressing issues, and introducing new features. By analyzing developer contributions, code updates, and activity on platforms like GitHub, investors can gauge the project's technical progress and the engagement of its development team. A strong and consistent level of developer activity suggests that the project is evolving to meet market demands and address challenges.

The quality and transparency of the development team are equally important. Projects with experienced and reputable developers are more likely to succeed, as their expertise instills confidence among investors and partners. Transparency, including open communication about roadmaps, milestones, and challenges, further enhances trust in the project. Conversely, a lack of visible developer activity or anonymous teams may raise red flags, signaling potential risks or a lack of accountability.

Token utility and adoption are fundamental to an altcoin's long-term success. A token's utility refers to its functional value within a blockchain ecosystem. Tokens that enable essential operations, such as powering smart contracts, facilitating transactions, or providing access to services, are more likely to sustain demand and retain value. Evaluating the scope and diversity of a token's use cases provides insight into its relevance and adaptability in a competitive market.

Adoption reflects the extent to which a token is being used by individuals, businesses, and developers. High levels of adoption indicate that the token is meeting user needs and gaining traction in real-world applications. This metric is often evidenced by partnerships, integrations, and the number of active users within the project's ecosystem. Altcoins with robust adoption demonstrate the ability to scale and attract diverse stakeholders, ensuring their relevance and resilience over time.

For example, altcoins that power decentralized finance (DeFi) platforms often have strong utility and adoption. These tokens are used for governance, liquidity provision, or staking, creating multiple layers of demand. The success of such altcoins depends on the growth of their underlying platforms and the ability to maintain active and engaged communities. Evaluating token utility and adoption alongside market metrics provides a comprehensive understanding of an altcoin's potential.

Community engagement also plays a critical role in evaluating altcoin projects, making readers feel included and part of a larger movement. A vibrant and active community indicates widespread support and interest in the project. Communities contribute to the growth and visibility of altcoins through advocacy, development contributions, and user adoption. Social media presence, participation in forums, and attendance at events are measurable indicators of community strength. Projects with strong communities are better positioned to weather market fluctuations and sustain momentum over the long term.

Regulatory compliance is an increasingly important factor in evaluating altcoin projects, providing readers with a sense of security and confidence in their investments. As governments and regulatory bodies scrutinize the cryptocurrency industry, projects must navigate complex legal landscapes to ensure compliance with local and international laws. Regulatory clarity enhances investor confidence and reduces the risk of legal challenges that could disrupt a project's operations. Altcoins that proactively address compliance issues and adopt transparent practices are more likely to attract institutional and retail investors.

An altcoin project's underlying technology and scalability are also crucial to its evaluation. Scalability refers to a blockchain's ability to handle a growing number of transactions and users without compromising speed or efficiency. Projects prioritizing scalability often employ innovative technologies, such as layer-2 solutions or sharding, to enhance their networks. Evaluating an altcoin's scalability provides insights into its capacity to support widespread adoption and sustain growth.

Security is another critical aspect of technology evaluation. Altcoins' robust security measures, including resistance to attacks and vulnerabilities, inspire confidence among users and investors. Audits, bug bounty programs, and partnerships with cybersecurity firms are indicators of a project's commitment to safeguarding its network. Projects that need to address security concerns risk losing credibility and market value.

Partnerships and collaborations further influence the evaluation of altcoin projects. Strategic alliances with established organizations or blockchain platforms enhance credibility and expand the altcoin's reach. Partnerships often lead to integrations, co-development initiatives, and increased visibility, driving adoption and utility. Assessing the quality and scope of a project's partnerships provides valuable context for its market position and potential.

Evaluating altcoin projects requires a multifaceted approach considering key metrics, market dynamics, development activity, utility, and adoption. By analyzing these factors holistically, investors and stakeholders can identify promising opportunities while mitigating risks. The rapidly evolving nature of the cryptocurrency market demands continuous monitoring and adaptation, ensuring that altcoin evaluations remain relevant and informed. In this dynamic environment, a thorough and nuanced understanding of altcoin projects is essential for navigating the complexities and unlocking the potential of the digital asset landscape.

Evaluating an altcoin project involves a systematic approach to assessing its potential, risks, and alignment with an investor's goals. Here's a practical example using a hypothetical altcoin project: EcoChain, which claims to be a blockchain platform focused on sustainability and green energy initiatives.

## Step 1: Assess Key Metrics

The first step in evaluating EcoChain is analyzing its fundamental metrics to understand its market dynamics and position. The investor reviews:

**Market Capitalization:** EcoChain's market cap is $500 million. This places it in the mid-tier range among altcoins, signaling growth potential but indicating moderate risk compared to more established cryptocurrencies.

**Circulating Supply:** Out of 1 billion tokens, 700 million are already in circulation. This suggests that while a significant portion of tokens is in the market, additional issuance could dilute value if demand doesn't grow proportionately.

**Trading Volume:** The daily trading volume averages $30 million, demonstrating decent liquidity. This means the token is actively traded, reducing illiquidity risk when exiting positions.

## Step 2: Examine Developer Activity

The investor checks developer activity on platforms like GitHub, where the EcoChain team publicly shares code updates and progress. The repository has shown consistent updates over the past six months, with new features like an advanced staking mechanism and improvements to transaction speeds. A detailed roadmap outlines upcoming features such as partnerships with renewable energy providers.

The investor notes that the team has disclosed its identities and backgrounds, including engineers with prior experience at reputable blockchain firms. Transparency and expertise enhance trust in the project's longevity and capability to execute its vision.

### Step 3: Evaluate Token Utility and Adoption

EcoChain's token, ECO, has clear utility within the ecosystem. Users can stake ECO tokens to participate in network governance, pay for transactions, and access blockchain-generated green energy data. The token also supports a carbon offset program, where a portion of transaction fees funds reforestation projects.

Adoption metrics show that over 100 renewable energy firms use EcoChain to tokenize their energy credits. Additionally, several decentralized applications (dApps) built on EcoChain have attracted a modest but growing user base, reflecting real-world adoption. The investor cross-references these claims with independent blockchain analytics platforms to confirm user activity.

### Step 4: Analyze Community Engagement

The investor explores EcoChain's social media platforms, online forums, and community events. The project's Twitter account has 150,000 followers, and its Reddit forum has 25,000 active members. The community frequently engages with updates, contributing ideas for new features and advocating for EcoChain's mission. This engagement indicates a strong, supportive user base, often critical for long-term success. EcoChain's development team also hosts monthly AMAs (Ask Me Anything) sessions, reinforcing transparency and strengthening ties with the community.

## Step 5: Review Partnerships and Collaborations

EcoChain has partnered with two prominent renewable energy companies and one blockchain analytics firm. These collaborations enhance the platform's credibility and expand its potential use cases. The investor also notes that EcoChain has received grants from a government clean energy initiative, further validating its commitment to sustainability and aligning it with broader regulatory goals.

## Step 6: Assess Risks

Despite its potential, the investor identifies risks:

**Regulatory Uncertainty:** As a blockchain project targeting the energy sector, EcoChain may face scrutiny over its compliance with environmental and financial regulations.

**Competition:** Other projects, such as Algorand and Energy Web Token, are competing in the sustainability niche, requiring EcoChain to differentiate itself continuously.

**Technology Maturity:** The platform is still in its early stages, with inherent risks of bugs, delays, or failure to meet roadmap milestones.

## Step 7: Make an Informed Decision

After this evaluation, the investor concludes that EcoChain shows promise due to its clear utility, strong community engagement, and meaningful partnerships. However, the identified risks mean that investment should be approached with caution. The investor decides to allocate a small portion of their portfolio to ECO tokens, with plans to monitor progress on developer activity, partnerships, and adoption metrics over the next six months.

This example highlights how a systematic evaluation process can help investors and stakeholders make informed decisions about altcoin projects, balancing potential rewards with associated risks.

## Understanding Tokenomics

Tokenomics, the economic design behind a cryptocurrency, is one of the most critical aspects of evaluating and understanding an altcoin project. It refers to the framework that governs how tokens are created, distributed, and utilized within a blockchain ecosystem. Effective tokenomics ensures that a project's economic model aligns with its goals, incentivizes participation, and supports sustainable growth. Understanding key concepts such as supply mechanisms, inflation versus deflationary models, and incentive structures provides a comprehensive perspective on the value and viability of a cryptocurrency.

Supply mechanisms form the foundation of tokenomics, determining how tokens are issued and circulated within a project's ecosystem. These mechanisms balance token availability and demand, ensuring the token retains its value over time. Some projects opt for a fixed supply, where the total number of tokens is predetermined and cannot be increased. This scarcity-driven model is commonly associated with projects like Bitcoin, whose maximum supply is capped at 21 million tokens. The idea is to replicate the scarcity of valuable resources such as gold, driving demand as the supply diminishes over time.

Other projects adopt a dynamic supply model, where tokens are issued or burned based on specific conditions or rules. This approach offers flexibility and allows projects to respond to changes in demand or market conditions. For instance, a project might issue new tokens to reward users or burn tokens to reduce supply and stabilize prices. Dynamic supply mechanisms can also include token buybacks, where the project uses revenue to purchase tokens from the market and remove them from circulation. This mechanism enhances scarcity and signals confidence in the project's value.

Another critical aspect of tokenomics is the distinction between inflationary and deflationary models. Inflationary models introduce new tokens into the ecosystem over time, often through mining, staking, or liquidity provision. This approach is designed to incentivize participation and maintain network security, particularly in the early stages of a project. By rewarding miners, validators, or liquidity providers with newly issued tokens, inflationary models encourage users to contribute resources and support the network.

However, inflationary models come with the risk of token dilution, where the value of existing tokens decreases as new tokens are issued. To mitigate this, projects must carefully manage the inflation rate and ensure that demand keeps pace with supply. A well-executed inflationary model can strike a balance between incentivizing participation and preserving token value, creating a sustainable ecosystem that supports long-term growth.

Deflationary models, on the other hand, reduce the token supply over time, often through mechanisms like token burning. In these models, a portion of tokens is permanently removed from circulation, creating scarcity and potentially driving up the value of the remaining tokens. Deflationary models are popular among projects that prioritize value appreciation and align tokenomics with investor interests. For example, some decentralized finance (DeFi) platforms implement deflationary mechanisms by burning a percentage of transaction fees, rewarding token holders with increased value as the supply diminishes.

Both inflationary and deflationary models have advantages and challenges, and the choice between them depends on the project's goals and use cases. Inflationary models are well-suited for projects that rely on active participation and network growth, as they provide ongoing incentives for users and contributors. Deflationary models, by contrast, appeal to projects focused on creating long-term value and rewarding token holders for their loyalty and investment.

Incentive structures are another cornerstone of tokenomics, driving user behavior and aligning stakeholder interests within a blockchain ecosystem. Incentives are designed to encourage participation, enhance security, and ensure the smooth functioning of the network. Projects use a variety of incentive mechanisms, including staking rewards, governance participation, liquidity provision, and ecosystem contributions, to motivate users and contributors.

Staking rewards are a common incentive in proof-of-stake (PoS) networks. Users lock up their tokens to participate in validating transactions and securing the network. In return, they receive rewards through newly issued tokens or transaction fees. Staking incentivizes users to support the network and aligns their interests with its success, as their rewards depend on the network's health and stability.

Governance participation is another important incentive, particularly in decentralized autonomous organizations (DAOs) and blockchain platforms with on-chain governance. Token holders are encouraged to vote on proposals, shape the project's direction, and contribute to decision-making processes. By giving users a voice in governance, projects foster a sense of ownership and accountability, ensuring that the ecosystem evolves in line with community priorities.

Liquidity provision incentives are widely used in DeFi platforms, where users supply tokens to liquidity pools in exchange for rewards. These incentives are critical for ensuring the availability of assets within decentralized exchanges and lending platforms, enabling seamless transactions and efficient market operations. Liquidity providers are typically rewarded with a share of transaction fees or governance tokens, creating a symbiotic relationship between users and the platform.

Ecosystem contributions, such as creating content, developing applications, or promoting adoption, are also incentivized in many blockchain projects. Projects encourage active participation and community engagement by rewarding users for their contributions, driving growth and visibility. These incentives often take the form of token airdrops, grants, or revenue-sharing programs, ensuring that contributors are fairly compensated for their efforts.

The effectiveness of incentive structures depends on their design and alignment with the project's goals. Poorly designed incentives can lead to unintended consequences, such as excessive speculation, unsustainable inflation, or stakeholder misalignment. For example, if staking rewards are too high, they may encourage hoarding rather than active participation, undermining the network's functionality. Similarly, if liquidity provision incentives are not carefully calibrated, they may lead to market distortions or excessive reliance on external incentives.

Transparency and communication are essential for ensuring that the community understands and accepts incentive structures. Projects that clearly explain their tokenomics, including the rationale behind supply mechanisms, inflation or deflation models, and incentive structures, are more likely to gain trust and attract long-term participants. Regular updates, audits, and open discussions further enhance transparency, ensuring tokenomics remains aligned with the project's goals and evolving market conditions.

Tokenomics is a dynamic and complex field that plays a critical role in the success of altcoin projects. By understanding supply mechanisms, inflation versus deflationary models, and incentive structures, stakeholders can gain valuable insights into a project's potential and sustainability. Effective tokenomics support the functionality and growth of blockchain ecosystems and align the interests of developers, users, and investors, creating a foundation for long-term success. As the cryptocurrency market continues to evolve, the importance of well-designed tokenomics will only grow, shaping the future of digital assets and decentralized technologies.

## Red Flags To Avoid

The explosive growth of the cryptocurrency market has attracted diverse projects, ranging from transformative innovations to opportunistic scams. For investors, developers, and enthusiasts, identifying red flags is crucial for navigating this landscape and making informed decisions. Understanding common warning signs, such as vaporware projects, poor governance models, and a lack of transparency, can help stakeholders distinguish legitimate opportunities from potential pitfalls. By recognizing these red flags, participants can mitigate risks and contribute to a healthier and more trustworthy ecosystem.

One of the most prevalent red flags in the cryptocurrency space is the phenomenon of vaporware projects. These projects promise groundbreaking innovations or revolutionary solutions but need more substance, development, or expertise to deliver on their claims. Vaporware projects often rely on exaggerated marketing campaigns, buzzwords, and flashy presentations to attract attention and funding. However, closer inspection reveals a need for tangible progress, meaningful milestones, or working prototypes.

Vaporware projects thrive on hype, creating unrealistic expectations about their potential impact. They often emphasize future possibilities rather than present realities, deflecting scrutiny with promises of forthcoming breakthroughs. While it is not uncommon for early-stage blockchain projects to operate with incomplete products or ambitious goals, the key distinction lies in a clear roadmap, a credible development team, and consistent updates. Projects that need to demonstrate progress over time, complete deadlines without explanation, or avoid releasing details about their technology should raise serious concerns.

The motivations behind vaporware projects can vary. In some cases, they result from overambitious founders who need more technical expertise or resources to execute their vision. In more concerning instances, vaporware is a deliberate scam designed to exploit investor enthusiasm and secure funding without any intention of delivering a viable product. These projects often conduct aggressive token sales or initial coin offerings (ICOs), collecting large sums of money before disappearing with investors' funds.

Identifying vaporware requires careful due diligence. Reviewing a project's whitepaper, technical documentation, and development progress can reveal inconsistencies or unrealistic claims. Engaging with the community and observing how the team communicates can provide valuable insights into the project's legitimacy. Projects that prioritize transparency, openly acknowledge challenges and demonstrate measurable progress are far less likely to be classified as vaporware.

Poor governance models are another significant red flag in cryptocurrency projects. Governance refers to the mechanisms and processes that guide decision-making, resource allocation, and conflict resolution within a blockchain ecosystem. Effective governance is critical for ensuring that projects evolve in alignment with their goals and community interests. However, poorly designed or implemented governance models can lead to inefficiency, centralization, and a lack of accountability.

Centralized governance is a common issue where small individuals or entities hold disproportionate control over the project. This concentration of power undermines the decentralized ethos of blockchain technology and creates risks of manipulation or self-serving behavior. For example, if a project's founders or early investors retain excessive influence over governance decisions, they may prioritize short-term gains over long-term sustainability or community welfare.

On the other hand, governance that is overly decentralized and needs a clear structure can lead to decision-making paralysis and inefficiency. With defined processes for proposing and implementing changes, communities may be able to reach consensus or execute critical updates. This stagnation can hinder a project's ability to adapt to market conditions, address challenges, or innovate effectively.

Governance models should be transparent, inclusive, and adaptable. Projects that need to define their governance structure or provide opportunities for community participation risk alienating their user base and eroding trust. The absence of governance documentation, voting mechanisms, or clear accountability measures should be considered a red flag, as it indicates a lack of foresight or commitment to sustainable growth.

The role of token distribution in governance must be considered. Projects, where a significant portion of tokens is concentrated among founders, developers, or early investors, may create power imbalances that skew decision-making. Fair and equitable token distribution ensures that governance power is distributed among diverse stakeholders, fostering inclusivity and reducing the risk of manipulation.

Lack of transparency is one of the most damaging red flags in cryptocurrency projects. Transparency is a cornerstone of trust, particularly in decentralized ecosystems where participants rely on open and verifiable information to make decisions. Projects that withhold information obscure their operations or fail to communicate effectively, creating an environment of uncertainty and suspicion.

A lack of transparency can manifest in several ways. Teams that operate anonymously or use pseudonyms without providing verifiable credentials raise concerns about accountability. While anonymity can be justified in some cases, such as protecting privacy in politically sensitive regions, it should be accompanied by strong assurances of legitimacy and credibility. Projects that avoid revealing the identities of their founders, developers, or advisors may need more accountability, making it easier for stakeholders to hold them responsible for their actions.

Transparency also extends to financial practices. Projects that do not disclose how funds are allocated, spent, or managed invite skepticism about their intentions. For example, a project that raises significant capital through an ICO or token sale needs to provide detailed reports on fund usage risks being perceived as dishonest or poorly managed. Regular financial audits, detailed expenditure reports, and independent oversight enhance trust and demonstrate a commitment to responsible stewardship.

Communication is another critical aspect of transparency. Projects that maintain an open dialogue with their community provide regular updates and address concerns proactively are more likely to gain and retain trust. Conversely, projects that ignore questions provide vague or inconsistent information or avoid discussing setbacks may attempt to obscure underlying issues. Clear, consistent, and honest communication is essential for building confidence and fostering a loyal user base.

Transparency is particularly important during periods of crisis or controversy. How a project handles challenges, such as security breaches, regulatory scrutiny, or market downturns, speaks volumes about its integrity and resilience. Projects that address issues openly take responsibility and implement corrective measures demonstrate accountability and commitment to their stakeholders. In contrast, projects that deflect blame, downplay problems or refuse to engage with their community risk losing credibility and support.

Recognizing red flags such as vaporware projects, poor governance models, and lack of transparency is crucial for navigating the cryptocurrency market and avoiding potential pitfalls. These warning signs highlight fundamental weaknesses that can undermine a project's credibility, sustainability, and value. By conducting thorough due diligence, engaging with the community, and demanding transparency, participants can make informed decisions and contribute to a healthier and more trustworthy ecosystem. Awareness of these red flags empowers investors and stakeholders to support projects that prioritize integrity, innovation, and accountability, fostering the long-term success of the cryptocurrency industry.

# CHAPTER 10: REGULATION AND LEGAL TRENDS

*"Regulation is necessary for the crypto market to mature." — Brad Garlinghouse.*

Garlinghouse's assertion reflects the critical role that regulation plays in the evolution of the cryptocurrency market. Clear and consistent regulatory frameworks are essential for altcoins to move beyond their speculative origins and achieve widespread adoption. The regulation provides legal clarity for investors, developers, and institutions to operate confidently in the altcoin ecosystem. The absence of regulation can lead to uncertainty, fraud, and instability, deterring potential investors and undermining trust in the market. By establishing rules that protect participants while fostering innovation, regulators can create an environment where altcoins can thrive. For example, distinguishing between utility tokens and securities ensures that projects with legitimate use cases are not hindered by excessive oversight, while fraudulent schemes face stricter scrutiny.

Regulation also paves the way for institutional adoption, as compliance requirements often hinder large-scale investment. Institutions need assurance that their activities align with legal standards, and regulatory clarity can facilitate their entry into the altcoin space. This dynamic is critical as altcoins seek to integrate with traditional financial systems and expand their influence. Garlinghouse's perspective highlights the balance between innovation and compliance. While excessive regulation could stifle creativity, thoughtful policies can enable the altcoin market to mature and achieve its potential as a transformative force in the global economy.

Cryptocurrency, once operating on the fringes of financial systems, has evolved into a global phenomenon that touches nearly every industry. This rise has brought increased scrutiny from governments and regulatory bodies worldwide. Regulation and legal frameworks are critical for shaping the future of cryptocurrencies, including altcoins. Striking the right balance between fostering innovation and ensuring compliance has become a central challenge for policymakers and industry stakeholders. Understanding crypto regulation worldwide, key regulatory frameworks, crypto-friendly jurisdictions, and the ongoing effort to balance innovation and compliance provides insight into the evolving legal landscape and inspires excitement about the potential of blockchain technology.

Crypto regulation varies significantly across countries, reflecting economic priorities, political ideologies, and technological adoption differences. Some nations have embraced cryptocurrency as a driver of innovation and economic growth, creating favorable regulatory environments to attract blockchain businesses and investments. Others have cautiously approached cryptocurrencies, citing financial stability, illicit activities, and consumer protection concerns. This patchwork of regulations has created a complex global landscape that influences how cryptocurrencies are adopted and used.

In countries like the United States, crypto regulation is fragmented and evolving. Multiple regulatory agencies, including the Securities and Exchange Commission (SEC), Commodity Futures Trading Commission (CFTC), and Financial Crimes Enforcement Network (FinCEN), oversee various aspects of the cryptocurrency market. The SEC has focused on determining whether specific tokens qualify as securities, applying existing securities laws to blockchain-based assets. Meanwhile, the CFTC regulates derivatives markets for cryptocurrencies like Bitcoin and Ethereum. FinCEN emphasizes anti-money laundering (AML) compliance and the enforcement of know-your-customer (KYC) requirements for crypto exchanges and financial institutions.

In contrast, the European Union (EU) has sought to harmonize cryptocurrency regulation across member states. The proposed Markets in Crypto-Assets (MiCA) regulation aims to provide a comprehensive framework for issuing and trading cryptocurrencies and stablecoins. MiCA introduces rules for token issuers, exchanges, and service providers, emphasizing transparency, consumer protection, and financial stability. The EU seeks to balance innovation with safeguards against systemic risks by creating a unified regulatory environment.

In Asia, regulatory approaches to cryptocurrency range from permissive to prohibitive. Japan is considered a pioneer in crypto regulation, having legalized cryptocurrencies as a form of payment in 2017 and implementing robust oversight for exchanges. The country's regulatory framework emphasizes consumer protection and operational security, fostering trust in the market. On the other hand, China has adopted a restrictive stance, banning cryptocurrency trading and mining while promoting its central bank digital currency (CBDC), the digital yuan. Singapore represents a middle ground, offering a supportive environment for blockchain innovation under its Payment Services Act while maintaining strict compliance standards for AML and counter-terrorism financing (CTF).

Key regulatory frameworks shape how cryptocurrencies are developed, traded, and integrated into the global economy. These frameworks address critical issues such as securities classification, taxation, AML compliance, and consumer protection. Classifying cryptocurrencies as securities, commodities, or currencies is pivotal in determining how they are regulated. Projects that issue tokens resembling investment contracts may be subject to securities laws, requiring registration, disclosures, and compliance with investor protection standards.

Taxation frameworks for cryptocurrencies vary widely, with some countries treating them as assets subject to capital gains taxes and others applying income tax to crypto earnings. Transparent and consistent tax policies are essential for fostering compliance and reducing uncertainty for investors and businesses. In jurisdictions with unclear or punitive tax regimes, the risk of non-compliance increases, potentially stifling growth and innovation.

AML and KYC requirements are foundational to crypto regulation, aiming to prevent the misuse of cryptocurrencies for illicit activities such as money laundering, tax evasion, and terrorist financing. These requirements mandate that crypto exchanges and service providers verify the identities of their users, monitor transactions, and report suspicious activities. While AML and KYC measures enhance transparency and accountability, they also raise concerns about privacy and the potential exclusion of unbanked or underbanked populations from the crypto ecosystem.

Consumer protection is another critical aspect of regulatory frameworks. The volatile nature of cryptocurrencies and the prevalence of scams and frauds underscore the need for safeguards that protect retail investors. Regulatory measures such as licensing requirements for exchanges, custody rules, and dispute resolution mechanisms aim to create a safer environment for crypto users. At the same time, overly restrictive regulations may hinder access to legitimate opportunities, highlighting the need for a balanced approach that prioritizes consumer protection.

Crypto-friendly jurisdictions have emerged as hubs for blockchain innovation, attracting entrepreneurs, developers, and investors with supportive policies and infrastructure. These jurisdictions recognize cryptocurrencies' economic and technological potential and have crafted regulatory environments that foster growth while addressing key risks. Examples of crypto-friendly jurisdictions include Switzerland, Malta, and Estonia.

Switzerland, often called "Crypto Valley," is renowned for its progressive approach to blockchain regulation. The Swiss Financial Market Supervisory Authority (FINMA) provides clear guidelines for token classifications and ICOs, offering legal certainty for blockchain projects. The country's decentralized political system and favorable tax policies enhance its appeal to crypto businesses. The city of Zug, in particular, has become a global hub for blockchain companies and organizations, fostering a vibrant ecosystem of innovation and collaboration.

Malta, branded as the "Blockchain Island," has established itself as a leader in blockchain regulation by enacting comprehensive legal frameworks for cryptocurrencies and distributed ledger technology (DLT). The Malta Digital Innovation Authority oversees blockchain projects, ensuring compliance with technical and ethical standards. The country's proactive stance has attracted major crypto exchanges and startups, boosting its reputation as a global blockchain hub.

Estonia is another crypto-friendly jurisdiction that leverages its digital-first governance model to support blockchain innovation. The country offers e-residency programs that allow entrepreneurs to establish and manage blockchain businesses remotely. Estonia's transparent regulatory framework and emphasis on digital identity and cybersecurity create a conducive environment for blockchain adoption.

Balancing innovation and compliance is the central challenge for regulators and policymakers as they seek to integrate cryptocurrencies into the global financial system. On the one hand, overly restrictive regulations risk stifling innovation, driving blockchain projects and investments to more permissive jurisdictions. On the other hand, a lack of oversight can lead to market instability, fraud, and systemic risks that undermine trust in cryptocurrencies.

Striking this balance requires collaboration between regulators, industry stakeholders, and international organizations. Dialogue and partnerships can help align regulatory goals with the realities of blockchain technology, ensuring that frameworks are both effective and adaptable. For example, regulatory sandboxes, which allow blockchain projects to operate in controlled environments to test their innovations while adhering to compliance standards, are a practical solution. These sandboxes foster experimentation and innovation without compromising consumer protection or financial stability.

Transparency and clarity in regulatory approaches are essential for fostering trust and compliance. Ambiguity or inconsistency in regulations creates uncertainty for blockchain projects and investors, hindering growth and adoption. Clear guidelines for token classifications, taxation, and operational requirements enable businesses to navigate the regulatory landscape confidently. International cooperation is also critical for addressing cross-border challenges, such as money laundering and tax evasion, that require coordinated efforts and shared standards.

The evolving regulatory landscape highlights the importance of adaptability and innovation in policy design. Blockchain technology is inherently dynamic, with new use cases and applications emerging rapidly. Regulators must remain responsive to these changes, updating frameworks to address novel challenges and opportunities. Engaging with blockchain communities and industry experts ensures that practical insights and technical expertise inform regulations.

The interplay between regulation and innovation will shape the future of cryptocurrencies, including altcoins. As governments and institutions recognize blockchain technology's transformative potential, they can craft regulatory environments that support growth, stability, and inclusion. By balancing innovation and compliance, regulators can foster a thriving ecosystem that leverages the benefits of decentralization while addressing its risks and challenges. This delicate balance will determine how cryptocurrencies integrate into the broader economy, paving the way for a more inclusive and resilient financial future.

## Regulatory Risks For Altcoins

The rapidly growing world of altcoins faces significant regulatory risks that can shape their development, adoption, and market performance. These risks arise from the evolving legal and compliance landscape, often needing help keeping pace with blockchain technology's innovations and complexities. Among the most pressing challenges are the security versus utility token debate, the impact of government crackdowns, and the inherent uncertainty in regulatory frameworks. Navigating these risks requires a nuanced understanding of how regulation interacts with technological innovation and market dynamics.

The debate over whether an altcoin qualifies as a security or a utility token is one of the most contentious and consequential regulatory issues in the cryptocurrency space. This classification determines the legal obligations and compliance requirements that a project must meet, influencing its ability to raise funds, attract users, and operate within legal jurisdictions. The distinction between security and utility tokens often hinges on the token's purpose, use case, and the expectations of investors and regulators.

A security token represents an investment contract or financial asset, subjecting to securities laws and oversight by regulatory bodies like the U.S. Securities and Exchange Commission (SEC). Projects issuing security tokens must comply with strict disclosure, registration, and reporting requirements to protect investors and ensure market integrity. While these regulations aim to enhance transparency and trust, they can impose significant compliance costs and operational challenges on blockchain projects, potentially stifling innovation and limiting access to capital.

Utility tokens, on the other hand, are designed to provide access to a specific product, service, or ecosystem. They are not intended as investment vehicles and, in theory, fall outside the scope of securities regulations. However, the distinction is only sometimes clear-cut, and regulators may classify a utility token as a security if it is marketed or used in ways that create an expectation of profit. This ambiguity creates a gray area that complicates compliance for blockchain projects, particularly those seeking to balance token utility with investor appeal.

Different interpretations and regulatory approaches across jurisdictions further complicate the security versus utility token debate. In the United States, the Howey Test is often used to determine whether a token qualifies as a security. The test assesses whether an investment involves a common enterprise with an expectation of profits derived from the efforts of others. While the Howey Test provides a framework for analysis, its application to cryptocurrencies has led to inconsistent and subjective rulings, creating uncertainty for projects and investors.

In contrast, other jurisdictions, such as Switzerland, have introduced more nuanced frameworks that distinguish between payment, utility, and asset tokens. These classifications provide greater clarity for blockchain projects, enabling them to align their tokenomics and business models with regulatory expectations. However, the need for global harmonization in token classification remains a significant challenge, as projects operating across borders must navigate conflicting regulatory regimes and compliance requirements.

Government crackdowns on cryptocurrencies and blockchain projects represent another significant regulatory risk for altcoins. Governments often cite concerns about money laundering, tax evasion, consumer protection, and financial stability as reasons for imposing restrictive measures. These crackdowns can take various forms, including bans on cryptocurrency trading and mining, restrictions on initial coin offerings (ICOs), and heightened enforcement of anti-money laundering (AML) and know-your-customer (KYC) requirements.

China's comprehensive ban on cryptocurrency trading and mining is one of the most prominent examples of a government crackdown. The country's regulatory stance reflects its desire to maintain control over its financial system and promote its central bank digital currency (CBDC), the digital yuan. While the ban has driven crypto-related activities underground or offshore, it has also created significant disruptions for altcoin projects that previously relied on Chinese users, miners, or investors.

India has also grappled with regulatory uncertainty, with periodic proposals to ban or heavily regulate cryptocurrencies. Although outright bans have not materialized, the threat of restrictive legislation creates an atmosphere of caution and limits the growth of blockchain innovation in the region. Similarly, in the United States, increased scrutiny by regulatory agencies such as the SEC and the Commodity Futures Trading Commission (CFTC) has heightened compliance risks for altcoin projects, particularly those operating in the decentralized finance (DeFi) and initial token offering spaces.

Government crackdowns can have far-reaching consequences for altcoin markets. In addition to disrupting operations and liquidity, these measures often lead to declining investor confidence and market sentiment. Projects targeted by regulators may face legal challenges, penalties, or reputational damage, further eroding trust and value. Moreover, regulatory enforcement uncertainty challenges businesses and developers seeking to plan and scale their operations.

Despite these challenges, some altcoin projects have demonstrated resilience in the face of government crackdowns. By adapting to regulatory environments, diversifying their user bases, and fostering transparency, these projects have managed to maintain momentum and credibility. For example, projects that proactively comply with AML and KYC requirements or seek regulatory approvals often gain a competitive edge, attracting institutional investors and partners who value compliance and risk management.

Navigating the uncertainty of regulatory frameworks is the most pervasive challenge for altcoin projects. The cryptocurrency industry operates in a constantly evolving legal landscape where rules and interpretations can change rapidly. This uncertainty affects projects, users, investors, and other stakeholders, creating a sense of unpredictability that complicates decision-making and long-term planning.

For blockchain projects, regulatory uncertainty can manifest in several ways. In some cases, governments introduce ambiguous or overly broad regulations that fail to account for the nuances of blockchain technology. This lack of clarity leaves projects vulnerable to enforcement actions, even when they operate in good faith. In other cases, conflicting regulations across jurisdictions create a fragmented environment where compliance becomes costly and complex.

Investors and users also need help navigating regulatory uncertainty. The fear of legal repercussions or the potential for sudden changes in government policy can deter participation and investment in altcoin projects. Additionally, the lack of standardized regulations makes it difficult for stakeholders to assess blockchain initiatives' legitimacy and risk profile, hindering the broader adoption of cryptocurrencies.

To effectively navigate regulatory uncertainty, altcoin projects must adopt proactive and adaptive strategies. Engaging with regulators, industry associations, and legal experts helps projects stay informed about evolving requirements and advocate for fair and balanced policies. Transparency and communication are equally important, as they build trust with stakeholders and demonstrate a commitment to compliance and accountability.

Collaboration between regulators and the cryptocurrency industry is essential for reducing uncertainty and fostering innovation. Regulatory sandboxes, where blockchain projects can test their technologies in controlled environments, provide a valuable mechanism for balancing oversight with experimentation. These sandboxes enable regulators to understand blockchain applications better while allowing projects to refine their models and address compliance concerns.

The role of international cooperation in addressing the challenges of regulatory uncertainty cannot be overstated. Cryptocurrencies operate in a borderless environment, making it crucial for governments to coordinate their approaches and establish common standards. Initiatives such as the Financial Action Task Force (FATF) guidelines on cryptocurrency transactions represent a step toward global regulatory harmonization, reducing fragmentation and promoting consistency.

The regulatory risks facing altcoins, including the security versus utility token debate, government crackdowns, and regulatory uncertainty, highlight the complex interplay between innovation and compliance. While these risks present significant challenges, they also offer opportunities for projects to differentiate themselves through transparency, adaptability, and proactive engagement. By navigating these risks effectively, altcoins can position themselves as trusted and resilient players in the evolving cryptocurrency ecosystem, contributing to a more sustainable and inclusive digital economy.

## Emerging Legal Trends

As the cryptocurrency industry evolves, it faces a growing need to navigate the intersection of innovation and regulation. Emerging legal trends such as self-regulatory approaches, decentralized governance, and opportunities for advocacy are shaping how blockchain technology integrates into broader financial systems. These trends reflect an ongoing effort to address the challenges of regulatory oversight, compliance, and market trust while maintaining the core principles of decentralization and innovation.

Self-regulatory approaches are gaining traction as the cryptocurrency industry seeks to balance the need for oversight with the desire to maintain autonomy and flexibility. Self-regulation involves industry-led initiatives to establish standards, guidelines, and best practices that promote transparency, security, and accountability. By taking a proactive stance, the industry can address regulatory concerns while avoiding the imposition of overly restrictive government policies.

One of the driving forces behind self-regulatory approaches is the need to build trust and legitimacy. The early days of cryptocurrency were marred by high-profile scams, hacks, and frauds that eroded confidence among investors and regulators. Self-regulation allows industry participants to demonstrate their commitment to ethical behavior and consumer protection, fostering a more secure and reputable market environment.

Self-regulatory organizations (SROs) have emerged as key players in this effort. These bodies, often composed of blockchain companies, exchanges, and other stakeholders, develop and enforce rules that govern their members' activities. SROs work collaboratively with regulators, providing input on policy development and ensuring that industry standards align with legal requirements. This partnership enables the industry to influence regulatory frameworks while addressing potential risks and vulnerabilities.

One example of a successful self-regulatory initiative is the Crypto Rating Council (CRC), a consortium of cryptocurrency exchanges and financial firms. The CRC provides a standardized framework for assessing whether digital assets may qualify as securities under U.S. law. By offering clarity and consistency, the CRC helps projects and investors navigate the complexities of securities regulations, reducing uncertainty and fostering compliance.

Self-regulatory approaches also extend to technical standards and security practices. Initiatives such as the Decentralized Identity Foundation (DIF) focus on creating interoperable frameworks for digital identity, ensuring that blockchain-based systems meet privacy and security standards. These efforts highlight the industry's ability to address technical and ethical challenges without relying solely on government intervention.

While self-regulation offers many benefits, it has challenges. The cryptocurrency industry's decentralized nature makes it difficult to enforce standards uniformly, particularly in the absence of legal authority. Additionally, regulators may perceive self-regulatory efforts as insufficient and view them as an attempt to circumvent stricter oversight.

Striking a balance between self-regulation and external regulation is crucial for ensuring the industry remains innovative and accountable.

Decentralized governance is another emerging trend with profound implications for regulation and legal frameworks. It involves using blockchain technology and token-based voting systems to enable stakeholders to participate in decision-making. This model aligns with the principles of transparency, inclusivity, and decentralization that underpin blockchain technology, offering an alternative to traditional top-down regulatory approaches.

Decentralized autonomous organizations (DAOs) are at the forefront of decentralized governance. These blockchain-based entities operate without central control, relying on smart contracts and community-driven voting to make decisions. DAOs have been used to manage funds, develop protocols, and coordinate activities across various industries. Their governance models provide a framework for resolving disputes, allocating resources, and implementing changes in a decentralized manner.

One of the most significant implications of decentralized governance is its potential to address regulatory challenges. By enabling community participation and accountability, decentralized governance can enhance transparency and reduce the risk of fraud or misconduct. For example, DAOs can implement on-chain voting mechanisms that allow stakeholders to approve major decisions, such as protocol upgrades or funding allocations. These mechanisms ensure that decisions reflect the community's collective interests, fostering trust and legitimacy.

Decentralized governance also offers opportunities for self-regulation within the cryptocurrency industry. Projects can establish governance frameworks with rules and safeguards to address compliance, security, and ethical considerations. For instance, a DAO managing a decentralized finance (DeFi) platform could implement voting systems to approve new features or address vulnerabilities, ensuring that the platform evolves securely and responsibly.

Despite its potential, decentralized governance has challenges. The reliance on token-based voting can lead to power imbalances, where stakeholders with larger token holdings have disproportionate influence. Additionally, decentralized governance models may need help to adapt to rapidly changing regulatory landscapes, particularly when external authorities impose new requirements. Ensuring decentralized governance aligns with legal and ethical standards requires ongoing collaboration between blockchain communities, regulators, and industry leaders.

Opportunities for advocacy are crucial to the cryptocurrency industry's response to emerging legal trends. Advocacy involves engaging with policymakers, regulators, and the public to promote the benefits of blockchain technology and influence the development of fair and balanced regulations. By participating in advocacy efforts, industry stakeholders can ensure their voices are heard and their interests represented in the regulatory process.

One of the primary goals of advocacy is to educate policymakers and regulators about the complexities and potential of blockchain technology. Cryptocurrencies and decentralized systems should be more understood, leading to misconceptions and resistance among decision-makers. Advocacy organizations, industry associations, and think tanks are vital in bridging this knowledge gap, providing research, insights, and case studies highlighting blockchain innovation's positive impact.

Advocacy also involves building coalitions and partnerships to amplify the industry's voice. Collaborative efforts between blockchain companies, developers, investors, and academic institutions create a united front demonstrating the breadth and depth of support for cryptocurrency adoption. These coalitions can engage with international organizations, such as the Financial Action Task Force (FATF) or the World Economic Forum, to shape global standards and frameworks for blockchain regulation.

Grassroots advocacy is another powerful tool for influencing public opinion and policy development. Community-driven campaigns, petitions, and events raise awareness about the benefits of blockchain technology and mobilize support for favorable regulations. These efforts empower individual stakeholders to contribute to the industry's growth and sustainability, fostering a sense of ownership and accountability.

The role of advocacy extends beyond regulatory issues to broader societal challenges. Blockchain technology can potentially address pressing global problems, such as financial inclusion, data privacy, and climate change. Advocacy efforts highlighting these use cases demonstrate the technology's value and relevance, building support among diverse stakeholders. For example, promoting blockchain for sustainable supply chains or transparent governance can showcase its ability to drive positive change in critical areas.

Emerging legal trends in the cryptocurrency industry, including self-regulatory approaches, decentralized governance, and opportunities for advocacy, reflect the dynamic interplay between innovation and regulation. These trends highlight the industry's capacity to address challenges proactively while maintaining its core principles of decentralization and transparency. By embracing these approaches, stakeholders can navigate the complexities of the regulatory landscape, foster trust and accountability, and contribute to the sustainable growth of blockchain technology. As the industry evolves, these legal trends will be pivotal in shaping its future and ensuring its integration into the global economy.

# CHAPTER 11: RISKS AND CHALLENGES IN ALTCOIN INVESTMENT

*"Whenever the price of cryptocurrency is rallying, people start spending a lot more."* — Erik Voorhees.

Erik Voorhees, a renowned voice in the cryptocurrency world, draws attention to a common behavioral tendency among investors: the inclination to spend or invest more during market rallies. This phenomenon often stems from the psychological impact of rising prices, which can create an illusion of boundless opportunity. This behavior becomes even more pronounced in the altcoin market, characterized by its rapid price swings and speculative nature. When prices surge, many investors feel compelled to capitalize on perceived momentum quickly. This can lead to impulsive decisions, such as overleveraging, neglecting proper research, or investing in projects solely based on hype. These actions heighten the risk of significant losses, especially if a sudden market correction follows the rally. Voorhees' observation highlights the critical need for disciplined investment practices, even in the face of market exuberance.

Successful altcoin investing requires the ability to resist emotional reactions to price movements. Instead of succumbing to the euphoria of a rally, investors should focus on fundamentals, long-term goals, and risk management. Conducting thorough research, diversifying portfolios, and avoiding overcommitment are essential strategies for navigating the unpredictable nature of the altcoin market. Voorhees' insight is a powerful reminder that while market rallies may be exciting, they also come with heightened risks. Staying grounded and maintaining a clear strategy is key to making informed decisions and achieving sustainable success in the dynamic world of altcoin investments.

Altcoin investment offers the allure of exponential returns and the opportunity to participate in groundbreaking technologies. However, these opportunities come with significant risks and challenges. Market volatility, unpredictable price swings, correlation with Bitcoin movements, and the psychological pitfalls of emotional investing are among the key factors that make altcoin investment uniquely challenging. Navigating these risks requires a deep understanding of market dynamics, disciplined strategies, and emotional resilience. Being prepared for the emotional challenges of the altcoin market is key to your success.

Market volatility is a defining characteristic of the cryptocurrency market, and altcoins often experience even greater price fluctuations than Bitcoin or other established digital assets. This heightened volatility stems from several factors, including the relatively smaller market capitalizations of altcoins, speculative trading, and the nascent nature of the industry. Unlike traditional financial markets, which may move incrementally over weeks or months, altcoin prices can experience dramatic swings within hours or even minutes. This rapid movement creates both opportunities for profit and significant risks of loss.

The inherent volatility of altcoins can be attributed to their lower liquidity compared to major cryptocurrencies like Bitcoin and Ethereum. With fewer participants and trading volumes, altcoin markets are more susceptible to large price changes triggered by substantial buy or sell orders. For instance, a single whale transaction—a term used to describe large trades by individuals or institutions—can create dramatic upward or downward pressure on an altcoin's price. This lack of liquidity amplifies market instability, particularly for smaller or less well-known altcoins.

Speculation, a significant driver of market volatility, often leads many investors to the altcoin market in search of quick profits. This speculative behavior, often based on hype, rumors, or short-term trends, can cause rapid price movements as traders react to news, social media posts, or influencer endorsements. However, it's important to note that while speculative trading can yield significant gains during bull markets, it also heightens the risk of sudden crashes when sentiment shifts or news events create panic. This underscores the need for fundamental analysis over short-term trends.

Understanding altcoin price swings requires a deep dive into the underlying factors that influence market behavior. One of the primary contributors to price volatility is the early-stage nature of many altcoin projects. Unlike traditional stocks or bonds, which are often tied to established companies or governments, altcoins are frequently linked to blockchain projects that are still in development. This creates a high degree of uncertainty about their future success, leading to exaggerated market reactions to any updates, partnerships, or setbacks. Managing expectations and reactions to these updates is crucial in navigating the altcoin market.

Technological advancements or innovations can also drive significant price swings in altcoins. For example, releasing a major software upgrade or announcing a new use case can generate excitement and attract investors, leading to rapid price appreciation. Conversely, technical issues such as network downtime, security vulnerabilities, or delays in development can erode investor confidence and trigger sell-offs. This sensitivity to technological developments underscores the importance of thorough due diligence when investing in altcoins.

Regulatory news is another critical factor that

influences altcoin price movements. Announcements about government crackdowns, legal actions, or new regulations often create uncertainty in the market, prompting investors to react swiftly. For instance, a regulatory ban in one jurisdiction can lead to a global sell-off as traders fear broader implications for the industry. Conversely, favorable regulatory developments, such as approving a cryptocurrency-related product or supportive policy statements, can drive positive sentiment and price gains.

Market sentiment, shaped by social media, influencers, and online communities, is outsized in altcoin price swings. Platforms like Twitter, Reddit, and Telegram are hubs for discussions and speculation about cryptocurrency trends. A tweet from a high-profile figure or a viral post on a crypto forum can spark buying or selling frenzies, creating rapid and unpredictable price movements. While this dynamic can create lucrative opportunities for investors who act quickly, it also introduces significant misinformation and market manipulation risks.

Altcoin prices are often closely correlated with Bitcoin movements, reflecting Bitcoin's dominant role in the cryptocurrency ecosystem. As the first and most widely recognized cryptocurrency, Bitcoin is a benchmark for the entire market, influencing investor sentiment and market trends. When Bitcoin experiences significant price changes, altcoins typically follow suit, amplifying the broader market's volatility.

This correlation with Bitcoin can be both an advantage and a challenge for altcoin investors. On the one hand, it provides a degree of predictability, as movements in Bitcoin can indicate potential shifts in altcoin prices. For example, a Bitcoin rally often triggers increased interest in altcoins as investors seek to capitalize on broader market momentum. On the other hand, this correlation means that altcoins are vulnerable to external factors affecting Bitcoin, such as regulatory news, macroeconomic trends, or changes in institutional sentiment.

Understanding the nuances of this correlation requires analyzing how altcoins respond to Bitcoin movements in different market conditions. During bull markets, altcoins often experience amplified gains as investors diversify their portfolios and speculate on high-growth opportunities. However, altcoins tend to suffer more significant losses in bear markets, as their smaller market capitalizations and higher volatility make them more susceptible to downturns. This cyclical relationship underscores the importance of timing and market awareness in altcoin investment.

Managing emotional investing is one of the most challenging aspects of navigating the altcoin market. The rapid price movements and speculative nature of altcoins create an environment where fear and greed can dominate decision-making. These emotional responses often lead to impulsive actions, such as panic selling during market downturns or overextending positions during price surges. Recognizing and mitigating these tendencies is essential for maintaining discipline and achieving long-term success.

Fear of missing out (FOMO) is a common psychological pitfall in the altcoin market. When investors see others profiting from rapid price gains, they may feel pressured to enter the market without conducting proper research or considering the risks. This herd mentality often leads to buying at inflated prices, only to face losses when the market corrects. Developing a clear investment strategy and sticking to it, regardless of market hype, can help investors avoid the pitfalls of FOMO.

Similarly, fear, uncertainty, and doubt (FUD) can drive irrational selling during market downturns. Negative news, rumors, or market declines often create a sense of panic, leading investors to sell their holdings at a loss. This emotional reaction is compounded by the volatility of altcoins, where rapid price drops can create an illusion of impending collapse. Building emotional resilience and focusing on long-term goals rather than short-term fluctuations is crucial for navigating these challenges.

Discipline and risk management are essential tools for emotional investing in the altcoin market. Setting clear entry and exit points, diversifying investments, and adhering to stop-loss strategies can help investors maintain control over their decisions. Educating oneself about market dynamics, technical analysis, and project fundamentals also provides a foundation for making informed choices, reducing the influence of emotions on investment outcomes.

Market volatility, altcoin price swings, correlation with Bitcoin movements, and emotional investing are intertwined risks and challenges that define the altcoin market. While these factors create opportunities for significant returns, they also demand careful navigation, disciplined strategies, and emotional resilience. By understanding these dynamics and adopting a proactive approach to risk management, investors can position themselves to succeed in the fast-paced and unpredictable world of altcoins. The ability to balance ambition with caution and analysis with intuition is key to unlocking the potential of this dynamic market.

## The Rise and Collapse of Terra (LUNA)

An example of the risks and challenges inherent in altcoin investment can be seen in Terra's dramatic rise and fall (LUNA) and its algorithmic stablecoin TerraUSD (UST) in 2022. Once celebrated as a pioneering blockchain project with the potential to revolutionize decentralized finance, Terra's collapse highlights how quickly fortunes can change in the volatile world of cryptocurrency.

At its height, Terra seemed unstoppable. The project's unique algorithmic model aimed to keep UST pegged to the US dollar without relying on traditional reserves, drawing significant attention from investors. LUNA, the ecosystem's native token, surged to over $116 by April 2022, bolstered by glowing market sentiment and widespread adoption. Investors poured in, lured by the promise of innovation and high returns, with the total value locked in Terra's ecosystem exceeding $30 billion. It was hailed as a beacon of blockchain's potential for a time.

But Terra's foundation was more fragile than it appeared. In May 2022, during a broader market downturn, UST lost its peg to the dollar. This initial instability sparked panic among investors, leading to a massive sell-off of UST. Terra's algorithm, designed to stabilize UST by minting and burning LUNA tokens, became overwhelmed. As the system tried to correct itself, an exponential increase in LUNA's supply flooded the market, triggering a price collapse. Within days, LUNA's value fell from over $80 to less than a cent, wiping out billions of dollars.

The broader market's conditions exacerbated Terra's implosion. Bitcoin, which often serves as a market bellwether, was also experiencing a sharp decline, dragging altcoins down. Terra's fate was closely tied to this larger trend, highlighting how Bitcoin's movements can ripple through the entire cryptocurrency market. Investors drawn in by the promise of quick gains suddenly faced catastrophic losses, and the emotional toll was palpable. Many held onto their LUNA tokens, unable or unwilling to sell, hoping for a rebound that never came.

Terra's story illustrates the critical challenges of altcoin investment: extreme market volatility, the dangers of herd mentality, and the psychological toll of rapid losses. It also underscores the importance of understanding the fundamentals of any project, avoiding overexposure, and staying disciplined even during moments of hype. For all its potential, the altcoin market is fraught with uncertainty, and Terra serves as a sobering reminder of how quickly fortunes can shift in this unpredictable space.

## Scams And Fraudulent Projects

The rapid growth of the cryptocurrency market has attracted not only investors and innovators but also scammers and bad actors seeking to exploit its decentralized and largely unregulated nature. Scams and fraudulent projects have plagued the industry, causing significant financial losses and eroding participant trust. Among the most pervasive schemes are pump-and-dump tactics, fraudulent initial coin offerings (ICOs), and misinformation campaigns. Recognizing these threats and learning how to navigate them are essential skills for anyone participating in the altcoin space.

Pump-and-dump schemes have become one of the most notorious forms of manipulation in the cryptocurrency market. These schemes involve artificially inflating the price of a low-liquidity altcoin through coordinated buying and promotional efforts, creating a flurry of excitement and interest among retail investors. Once the price reaches a certain peak, the orchestrators sell off their holdings en masse, causing the price to crash and leaving unsuspecting investors with substantial losses.

These schemes are often organized in private groups or through online forums and social media platforms where participants agree to promote a specific altcoin. The tactics used to create hype can range from spreading false claims about the project's potential to leveraging the influence of prominent figures in the crypto community. The rapid price surge attracts new buyers, driven by the fear of missing out, further fueling the artificial demand. However, as soon as the orchestrators cash out, the market collapses, and the altcoin's value plummets, often to levels below its original price.

The appeal of pump-and-dump schemes lies in their simplicity and the promise of quick profits, but they are highly unethical and illegal in many jurisdictions. Identifying these schemes before falling victim requires vigilance and skepticism for the average investor. Unusually rapid price increases without corresponding news, technological advancements, or legitimate partnerships should be treated as warning signs. Projects with vague or non-existent roadmaps, anonymous teams, and an overwhelming focus on aggressive marketing rather than development are often linked to these schemes.

Fraudulent initial coin offerings (ICOs) are another common tactic scammers use to prey on unsuspecting investors. During the ICO boom of 2017-2018, many blockchain projects used this fundraising model to attract capital by selling tokens that would power their ecosystems. While ICOs offered a legitimate pathway for innovative projects to raise funds, the lack of regulation made them a breeding ground for fraud.

Scammers often create elaborate websites, whitepapers, and promotional materials to present their ICOs as groundbreaking ventures. These fraudulent projects typically promise unrealistic returns or revolutionary technologies with little technical feasibility. Sometimes, they plagiarize content or fabricate their teams and partnerships. Once they have collected funds from investors, these scammers disappear, leaving participants with worthless tokens and no recourse for recovery.

The infamous example of BitConnect is a stark reminder of how fraudulent ICOs operate. BitConnect marketed itself as an investment platform that promised extraordinary returns through an automated trading bot. It attracted thousands of investors and reached a market cap of over $2 billion before collapsing in 2018, revealed as a Ponzi scheme. Its failure led to widespread losses and further scrutiny of the cryptocurrency space.

Investors must exercise extreme caution to avoid falling victim to fraudulent ICOs. Thorough due diligence on the project's team, technology, and partnerships is crucial. Genuine projects are typically transparent about their development process and actively engage with their communities. Additionally, reputable ICOs often undergo audits or seek compliance with emerging regulatory standards to build trust with investors.

Staying informed and maintaining a healthy skepticism are key strategies for protecting oneself from scams and fraudulent projects in the altcoin market. Cryptocurrency's decentralized and rapidly evolving nature makes it an attractive target for misinformation and manipulation. Scammers exploit the complexity of blockchain technology and the need for widespread understanding to deceive even experienced investors.

Education is one of the most effective tools for combating scams. Understanding how blockchain technology works, the basics of tokenomics, and the common tactics scammers use can empower investors to make informed decisions. Resources such as educational platforms, reputable news outlets, and blockchain analytics tools provide valuable insights into the industry and individual projects. Engaging with knowledgeable communities and forums can help identify red flags and share information about potential scams.

Transparency is another critical factor in staying informed. Legitimate projects often go to great lengths to ensure their operations, finances, and progress are accessible to the public. This includes open-source code repositories, regular updates on development milestones, and active communication with stakeholders. Conversely, projects that lack transparency or refuse to answer questions about their operations should be approached cautiously.

Community engagement is a double-edged sword in the fight against scams. While active communities can be a positive sign of a project's legitimacy, scammers can also manipulate them to create an illusion of credibility. Astroturfing, where fake accounts or bots flood forums and social media with positive comments, is a common tactic to generate hype around fraudulent projects. Identifying genuine engagement versus manufactured enthusiasm requires careful observation and cross-referencing information from multiple sources.

Regulation is important in addressing scams and fraudulent projects but is not a panacea. The decentralized and borderless nature of cryptocurrency makes enforcement challenging, as scammers can operate from jurisdictions with lax oversight. However, introducing regulatory frameworks has begun to deter bad actors and provide clearer guidelines for legitimate projects. Initiatives such as the EU's Markets in Crypto-

Assets (MiCA) regulation and the SEC's enforcement actions against fraudulent ICOs demonstrate the potential for regulation to improve accountability in the cryptocurrency market.

The role of self-regulation within the industry is equally important. Blockchain projects, exchanges, and other stakeholders can take proactive measures to identify and eliminate scams. For example, platforms like Binance and Coinbase implement rigorous listing processes to ensure that only reputable tokens are traded on their platforms. Additionally, initiatives such as bug bounty programs and code audits enhance the security and integrity of blockchain projects, reducing the risk of exploits.

Ultimately, protecting oneself from scams and fraudulent projects requires a combination of vigilance, education, and critical thinking. The promise of high returns in the altcoin market can be enticing, but it is essential to approach investments with a clear understanding of the risks involved. By staying informed, conducting thorough research, and fostering a healthy skepticism, participants can navigate cryptocurrency's complex and dynamic world with confidence and resilience. Scams may remain a persistent challenge in the industry, but with the right tools and mindset, they can be mitigated, allowing legitimate innovation to flourish.

As an example of how scams and fraudulent projects can devastate investors, the story of BitConnect stands out as one of the most infamous cases in cryptocurrency history. BitConnect promised extraordinary returns through a lending program supposedly powered by an automated trading bot. Investors were lured with guarantees of daily profits and flashy marketing campaigns, fueling a frenzy of excitement. By 2017, BCC's token had a market cap exceeding $2 billion.

However, beneath the surface, BitConnect was little more than a sophisticated Ponzi scheme. The company provided no evidence of its trading bot, and critics warned that returns were likely funded by new investors rather than legitimate profits. In early 2018, the platform abruptly shut down after regulators issued cease-and-desist orders. The value of BCC tokens plummeted to near zero, leaving thousands of investors with massive losses.

The collapse of BitConnect is a cautionary tale about the dangers of promises that seem too good to be true. It highlights the importance of skepticism, research, and transparency when evaluating altcoin projects. By learning from this example, investors can better protect themselves from falling victim to similar scams in the unpredictable world of cryptocurrency.

## Technical Challenges

The evolution of altcoins has been marked by remarkable innovation, but it has also exposed a series of technical challenges that developers, investors, and users must address. Among the most pressing are network security risks, smart contract vulnerabilities, and the need for effective scaling solutions. These challenges underscore the complexity of blockchain technology and highlight the importance of continued research, development, and vigilance.

Network security risks are a fundamental concern for any blockchain project, and altcoins are no exception. The decentralized nature of blockchain networks makes them robust against many traditional forms of attack, but it also introduces unique vulnerabilities. One of the most well-known threats is the 51% attack, where a malicious entity gains control of most of a network's computational power or staked tokens. With this majority control, attackers can manipulate the blockchain, reversing transactions, double-spending tokens, or disrupting network operations. The risk of such attacks is particularly acute for altcoins with smaller or less distributed networks, as they lack the computational or staking power to deter bad actors effectively.

The attack on Ethereum Classic in 2020 is a stark example of how a 51% attack can exploit network vulnerabilities. Attackers managed to reorganize the blockchain multiple times, enabling double-spending and damaging the network's reputation. Such incidents erode trust and can lead to sharp declines in an altcoin's value. Strengthening network security often requires incentivizing greater participation in mining or staking, adopting robust consensus mechanisms, and ensuring decentralization. However, achieving these goals can be resource-intensive and challenging, particularly for newer or smaller altcoins.

Another significant network security risk is the prevalence of Sybil attacks, where an attacker creates multiple identities or nodes to manipulate the network. This tactic can be used to influence consensus or governance decisions in proof-of-stake systems. Addressing Sybil attacks often involves implementing identity verification or resource-based constraints, but these measures must be balanced against the principles of decentralization and accessibility.

Smart contract vulnerabilities represent another critical technical challenge for altcoins. Smart contracts are self-executing programs that run on blockchain networks, automating transactions and other processes without intermediaries. While they offer significant benefits regarding efficiency and trustlessness, their complexity can introduce errors or loopholes that malicious actors can exploit. Even small bugs in a smart contract's code can have catastrophic consequences, leading to the loss of funds or the disruption of entire platforms.

The 2016 attack on The DAO, a decentralized autonomous organization built on Ethereum, is a seminal example of the risks posed by smart contract vulnerabilities. A flaw in The DAO's code allowed an attacker to siphon millions of dollars worth of ether, triggering a crisis that led to Ethereum's contentious hard fork. This incident demonstrated the high stakes of smart contract security and underscored the need for rigorous testing and auditing of code before deployment.

Auditing is now standard practice for most blockchain projects, with specialized firms examining smart contracts for vulnerabilities. However, audits are not foolproof, and the pace of innovation in the blockchain space often leads to deploying complex contracts that still need to be thoroughly vetted. To mitigate these risks, developers are increasingly adopting formal verification methods, where mathematical proofs are used to ensure the correctness of smart contracts. Despite these advances, the dynamic nature of blockchain technology means that new vulnerabilities can emerge as the ecosystem evolves.

Another challenge related to smart contract vulnerabilities is updating or modifying contracts once deployed. While the immutability of blockchain networks is a key feature, it can also be a drawback when it comes to fixing bugs or addressing unforeseen issues. Some projects have introduced upgradeable contracts or governance mechanisms that allow changes to be made, but these solutions often come with trade-offs in terms of complexity and security.

Scaling solutions are a pressing concern for altcoins, particularly as blockchain networks face increasing demand from users and applications. The ability to process transactions quickly, efficiently, and at low cost is critical for the success of any altcoin, yet many networks need help to achieve this balance. The underlying structure of most blockchains, which requires consensus among a distributed network of nodes, inherently limits scalability.

The scalability trilemma, a concept popularized by Ethereum's co-founder Vitalik Buterin, illustrates the challenge of balancing decentralization, security, and scalability. Most blockchain networks prioritize decentralization and security, but this often comes at the expense of scalability, leading to congestion, high fees, and slower transaction times during periods of high demand. Ethereum, for instance, has faced criticism for its scalability issues, particularly during the rise of decentralized finance (DeFi) and non-fungible tokens (NFTs), which placed immense strain on the network.

Various scaling solutions have been proposed and implemented to address these challenges. Layer 1 solutions involve changes to the blockchain's base protocol, such as increasing block sizes or implementing more efficient consensus mechanisms. For example, proof-of-stake (PoS) systems, like those adopted by Cardano and Solana, aim to improve scalability by reducing consensus's energy and computational requirements. However, transitioning to PoS can be complex and requires broad community support, as seen in Ethereum's long-awaited transition to Ethereum 2.0.

Layer 2 solutions represent another approach to scalability. In this approach, transactions are processed off-chain or on secondary layers, reducing the load on the main blockchain. Technologies like rollups, sidechains, and state channels allow for faster and cheaper transactions while maintaining the security of the underlying network. Polygon, for instance, has emerged as a popular Layer 2 solution for Ethereum, providing a scalable infrastructure for decentralized applications (dApps). While practical, these solutions introduce challenges, including interoperability and reliance on off-chain infrastructure.

Interoperability is a critical consideration for scaling solutions, as blockchain networks must be able to communicate and interact seamlessly to support a diverse ecosystem of applications. Projects like Polkadot and Cosmos focus on enabling interoperability through shared protocols and frameworks, allowing altcoins and dApps to scale without being confined to a single network. These innovations represent significant progress, but achieving true interoperability remains a complex technical and logistical challenge.

The development of scaling solutions is further complicated by the need to address environmental concerns. Energy-intensive consensus mechanisms like proof-of-work (PoW) have been criticized for their carbon footprints, prompting many projects to explore more sustainable alternatives. This shift requires not only technical innovation but also stakeholder alignment and resource allocation as networks transition to greener and more efficient models.

Technical challenges such as network security risks, smart contract vulnerabilities, and scalability are integral to the evolution of altcoins and the broader cryptocurrency ecosystem. Addressing these challenges requires rigorous development, collaboration, and continuous innovation. While the road ahead is fraught with difficulties, the progress made in overcoming these obstacles highlights the resilience and ingenuity of the blockchain community. By tackling these challenges head-on, altcoins can unlock their full potential and drive the next wave of technological and economic transformation.

# CHAPTER 12: BUILDING A DIVERSIFIED ALTCOIN PORTFOLIO

*"Diversification is protection against ignorance."*
— Warren Buffett.

Building a successful altcoin portfolio requires a careful balance of risk and reward, and diversification is a cornerstone of this strategy. Buffett's observation underscores the importance of spreading investments across multiple assets to mitigate the impact of market volatility and unforeseen challenges. A diversified portfolio provides stability and resilience in the altcoin market, where prices can swing dramatically.

Diversification involves selecting altcoins with different use cases, sectors, and risk profiles. For instance, a portfolio might include DeFi altcoins for financial innovation, gaming altcoins for exposure to the metaverse, and green altcoins for sustainable investing. This approach ensures that gains in one area can offset losses in another, creating a more balanced investment strategy.

Effective portfolio management also requires regular monitoring and rebalancing. Certain altcoins may outperform others as the market evolves, causing the portfolio to become skewed. Rebalancing helps maintain the desired allocation and ensures that the portfolio continues to align with the investor's goals. Buffett's insight reminds investors that diversification is not just a defensive strategy but a way to maximize opportunities. In a market as dynamic and diverse as altcoins, spreading investments across different projects and sectors is essential for navigating uncertainty and achieving long-term success.

The cryptocurrency market is thrilling, brimming with the potential for significant returns. However, this potential is accompanied by considerable risk. For investors eager to explore the volatile world of altcoins, constructing a diversified portfolio is a potent strategy that manages risk and maximizes opportunities. The process of developing a robust portfolio is an adventure in itself, involving:

- *Careful planning.*
- *Balancing risk and reward.*
- *Diversifying by use case.*
- *Deciding between long-term and short-term investment approaches.*

A diversified altcoin portfolio is more than just a collection of assets; it reflects an investor's goals, risk tolerance, and understanding of the market. Cryptocurrencies' unique characteristics shape portfolio strategies in the altcoin market. Unlike traditional financial markets, where assets often correlate with broader economic trends, altcoins exist where innovation, community sentiment, and technological developments play an outsized role. This dynamic requires a tailored approach to portfolio construction that accounts for the rapidly changing landscape and the diversity of projects within the ecosystem.

Understanding your risk tolerance is a pivotal starting point for building a portfolio. Some altcoins, particularly those with large market capitalizations and established use cases, are less volatile and carry lower risk. These assets, often called 'blue-chip altcoins,' include tokens like Ethereum, Cardano, and Solana. While they still exhibit price swings typical of cryptocurrencies, their established track records and ecosystems provide a measure of stability compared to smaller or newer projects. This understanding empowers you to make informed decisions about your investments.

Conversely, smaller-cap altcoins or those in their early stages offer higher potential returns but come with greater risk. These tokens may represent emerging technologies or niche markets that have yet to gain widespread adoption. While their upside can be significant, they are also more vulnerable to market fluctuations, regulatory scrutiny, and competition. Balancing these high-risk, high-reward assets with more stable investments is a fundamental aspect of a diversified altcoin portfolio.

Balancing risk and reward requires careful consideration of market conditions and individual project fundamentals. In bull markets, where sentiment is overwhelmingly positive, higher-risk altcoins often outperform as speculative interest drives their prices upward. In contrast, bear markets tend to favor more established cryptocurrencies, as investors seek refuge in assets perceived as safer. A diversified portfolio allows investors to benefit from both scenarios, smoothing out returns over time and reducing the impact of market volatility.

Understanding the specific use cases of altcoins is another key element of diversification. The cryptocurrency market encompasses various projects addressing different industries, technologies, and problems. By allocating funds across various use cases, investors can reduce their exposure to risks associated with any single sector while participating in the growth of multiple areas of innovation.

For instance, a well-diversified portfolio might include tokens that power decentralized finance (DeFi) platforms, such as Aave or Uniswap, alongside gaming and metaverse-related altcoins like Axie Infinity or Decentraland. It could also include infrastructure-focused tokens like Chainlink, which provides essential services to other blockchain networks, or privacy coins, such as Monero, which cater to users seeking secure and anonymous transactions. Each category of altcoins serves a unique function, and by investing across these categories, a portfolio captures the broader potential of blockchain technology.

Diversification by use case also allows investors to hedge against sector-specific risks. If regulatory changes negatively impact privacy coins, the portfolio's exposure to DeFi, gaming, or infrastructure projects may offset these losses. This approach mirrors the principles of traditional investment diversification, where assets in different industries or geographies are combined to reduce overall risk.

The decision between long-term and short-term investments further shapes a diversified altcoin portfolio. Long-term investments involve holding assets for extended periods, often years, to benefit from sustained growth and the compounding effects of innovation and adoption. This strategy is particularly effective for projects with strong fundamentals, robust development teams, and active communities. By focusing on long-term potential, investors can avoid the pitfalls of market timing and emotional decision-making, which often lead to poor outcomes in volatile markets.

Long-term investments also align with the development timelines of many blockchain projects.

Unlike traditional businesses, which may generate revenue and profits relatively quickly, blockchain initiatives often require years to achieve their goals. Projects focused on building new protocols, scaling solutions, or industry-specific applications may take time to gain traction, making patience a crucial component of long-term investing.

Short-term investments, on the other hand, aim to capitalize on market trends, price swings, and speculative opportunities. This approach requires a more active management style, as investors must monitor market movements, news, and technical indicators to identify profitable entry and exit points. While short-term trading can generate significant returns in the fast-paced altcoin market, it also carries higher risks and demands a deep understanding of market dynamics.

The choice between long-term and short-term investments often depends on an investor's time horizon, goals, and risk tolerance. A balanced portfolio, incorporating elements of both strategies, provides a sense of security. A core allocation to long-term holdings, supplemented by a smaller portion dedicated to short-term trades, allows investors to benefit from the stability and growth of established projects while taking advantage of short-term opportunities.

Risk management is critical in building and maintaining a diversified altcoin portfolio. The volatile nature of cryptocurrencies means that even well-constructed portfolios can experience significant fluctuations. Setting clear investment goals, determining appropriate position sizes, and establishing exit strategies are essential for navigating this volatility. Additionally, regular portfolio reviews help investors reassess their allocations and adjust based on market conditions or individual project performance changes.

The role of stablecoins in a diversified portfolio should not be overlooked. While not technically altcoins, stablecoins like USDC (a USD-backed stablecoin) or DAI (a decentralized stablecoin pegged to the US dollar) provide a valuable hedge against volatility. By allocating a portion of their portfolio to stablecoins, investors can protect their capital during market downturns and maintain liquidity for new opportunities. Stablecoins also facilitate participation in yield-generating activities, such as staking or lending, which can enhance returns without exposing the portfolio to excessive risk.

Building a diversified altcoin portfolio is both an art and a science, requiring a thoughtful approach to strategy, risk management, and market understanding. By balancing risk and reward, diversifying by use case, and integrating long-term and short-term investments, investors can navigate the complexities of the cryptocurrency market while positioning themselves for success. A well-constructed portfolio mitigates risks and captures the transformative potential of blockchain technology, offering a pathway to sustainable growth in this dynamic and rapidly evolving space.

## Top Tools For Altcoin Investors

Investing in altcoins requires more than intuition and market knowledge. The dynamic nature of the cryptocurrency market demands robust tools to track investments, analyze trends, and execute trades efficiently. Portfolio trackers, trading platforms, decentralized exchanges (DEXs), and analytics platforms have become indispensable for investors looking to navigate the complexities of altcoin investment. These tools streamline the investment process and empower investors with the insights and functionalities necessary to make informed decisions in a rapidly changing market.

Portfolio trackers are among the most essential tools for any altcoin investor. They provide a centralized way to monitor the performance of investments across various exchanges and wallets. With the proliferation of altcoins and the diverse ecosystems in which they operate, managing a portfolio can quickly become overwhelming without a tool to consolidate data. Portfolio trackers simplify this by aggregating real-time information about holdings, prices, and performance.

A good portfolio tracker lets investors view their holdings in one place, offering an overview of total value, individual asset performance, and historical trends. This consolidated view helps investors make strategic decisions about rebalancing, diversifying, or exiting positions. Some trackers also provide advanced features like profit and loss calculations, tax reporting, and alerts for significant market movements. These capabilities ensure that investors remain informed and respond swiftly to market changes.

In addition to tracking performance, portfolio trackers

often integrate with exchanges and wallets, making it easy to import transaction data. This seamless connectivity reduces manual entry and minimizes errors, which is particularly valuable for investors managing large or complex portfolios. Some platforms even support automated tracking of staking rewards, lending yields, or liquidity pool contributions, giving a comprehensive view of passive income streams.

Trading platforms and decentralized exchanges (DEXs) are equally critical for altcoin investors. These platforms facilitate the buying, selling, and swapping cryptocurrencies, serving as gateways to the altcoin market. The choice of trading platform depends on factors such as security, fees, user interface, and the range of supported altcoins. Centralized exchanges like Binance, Coinbase, and Kraken are popular among beginners for their accessibility, liquidity, and robust customer support. They often provide additional features such as staking, margin trading, and fiat on-ramps, making them versatile options for novice and experienced investors.

Decentralized exchanges, on the other hand, have gained prominence for their focus on privacy, security, and innovation. Platforms like Uniswap, PancakeSwap, and SushiSwap allow users to trade altcoins directly from their wallets, eliminating the need for a centralized intermediary. This peer-to-peer trading model is particularly appealing to investors who prioritize control over their funds and value the transparency of blockchain technology. DEXs often support a wider range of altcoins, including newly launched or niche tokens, providing opportunities to access projects not listed on centralized platforms.

The emergence of automated market makers (AMMs) has revolutionized the DEX landscape, enabling liquidity provision and trading without traditional order books. Investors can earn fees by participating in liquidity pools while facilitating decentralized trading. However, DEXs have challenges, such as higher transaction costs on congested networks like Ethereum and the risk of impermanent loss for liquidity providers. Choosing the right platform requires careful evaluation of these factors and alignment with investment goals.

Analytics and insights platforms provide the data and tools to understand market trends, evaluate altcoin projects, and identify opportunities. These platforms aggregate information from various sources, offering a comprehensive cryptocurrency landscape. For investors, access to reliable data is critical for making informed decisions and mitigating risks.

Market analytics platforms like CoinMarketCap and CoinGecko are widely used for their extensive data on altcoin prices, market capitalizations, trading volumes, and historical trends. These platforms provide snapshots of market performance and help investors compare assets across different metrics. They also offer insights into circulating supplies, project descriptions, and exchange listings, making them valuable resources for research and discovery.

Platforms like Messari and Glassnode delve into blockchain metrics, on-chain data, and fundamental analysis for more advanced analysis. These tools help investors understand network activity, token distribution, and developer engagement, providing a deeper perspective on project health and potential. For example, monitoring wallet activity can reveal trends in accumulation or distribution by large holders, while tracking transaction volumes offers clues about real-world adoption.

Decentralized finance (DeFi) analytics platforms, such as Dune Analytics and DeFi Pulse, focus on the rapidly growing ecosystem of decentralized applications. These platforms track metrics like total value locked (TVL), liquidity pool performance, and governance participation, enabling investors to assess the health and growth of DeFi projects. Understanding these metrics is essential for evaluating altcoins that power DeFi platforms, as they often reflect user adoption and network utility.

Social sentiment analysis has also emerged as a key tool for altcoin investors. Platforms like LunarCrush analyze social media activity, news, and influencer sentiment to gauge market psychology and identify emerging trends. In a market heavily influenced by community sentiment and hype, these insights can be instrumental in anticipating price movements or identifying projects gaining traction.

Integrating artificial intelligence (AI) and machine learning further enhances analytics capabilities. AI-powered tools can process vast amounts of data, identify patterns, and generate predictions, offering investors a competitive edge. For example, predictive algorithms can flag potential price breakouts or signal shifts in market sentiment, enabling timely decision-making.

Security is a critical consideration when selecting tools for altcoin investment. With the increasing prevalence of hacks, scams, and phishing attacks, ensuring the safety of funds and personal information is paramount. Many portfolio trackers, trading platforms, and analytics tools incorporate robust security measures, such as two-factor authentication, encryption, and cold storage solutions. However, users must also adopt best practices, such as using hardware wallets, avoiding suspicious links, and verifying the authenticity of platforms.

The interconnected nature of these tools highlights their role in creating a comprehensive investment ecosystem. Portfolio trackers help monitor performance, trading platforms enable transactions, and analytics tools provide the data for strategic decision-making. Together, they empower investors to navigate the complexities of the altcoin market with confidence and efficiency.

Building a reliable tool suite is an ongoing process that evolves alongside an investor's experience and goals. As the altcoin market grows and innovates, new tools and technologies will emerge, offering enhanced functionalities and insights. Staying informed about these developments and adapting to changes in the market is essential for maintaining a competitive edge.

The right tools simplify the investment process and unlock opportunities for growth and innovation. Investors can navigate the altcoin market with greater clarity and control by leveraging portfolio trackers, trading platforms, decentralized exchanges, and analytics tools. These tools represent the foundation of a successful investment strategy, enabling investors to thrive in cryptocurrency's dynamic and ever-changing world.

## Rebalancing And Exit Strategies

Effective rebalancing and exit strategies are vital to a successful altcoin investment plan. The cryptocurrency market's notorious volatility makes it essential for investors to regularly assess their portfolios, take profits strategically, and know when to exit poor-performing assets. These practices protect investments from unnecessary losses and position investors to capitalize on opportunities as market conditions evolve.

Reassessing investments is the cornerstone of maintaining a balanced and well-performing portfolio. The dynamic nature of the altcoin market means that projects, use cases, and market trends can change rapidly. What seemed like a promising investment six months ago might no longer align with an investor's goals or market realities. Regularly reviewing the fundamentals of each holding ensures that the portfolio remains aligned with an investor's strategy and risk tolerance.

Reassessment often begins with analyzing the performance and fundamentals of individual altcoins. Performance metrics such as price trends, trading volumes, and market capitalization can offer insights into how an altcoin is faring in the broader market.

For example, if an altcoin consistently underperforms despite favorable market conditions, it may indicate declining interest or unresolved issues within the project. On the other hand, strong performance may justify holding or even increasing an allocation.

Fundamentals provide a deeper layer of understanding. Assessing factors like development activity, partnerships, community engagement, and project roadmap updates reveals whether the underlying value proposition remains intact. For instance, a blockchain project consistently delivering on its promises and attracting developer interest is more likely to sustain long-term growth than one mired in delays or controversies. Reassessing investments this way allows investors to separate hype from genuine potential, enabling informed decision-making.

Market conditions are another critical factor to consider when reassessing investments. The altcoin market operates in cycles, with periods of bullish optimism followed by bearish corrections. During bull markets, reassessment may identify overvalued assets and consider profit-taking opportunities. In bear markets, the priority may shift to preserving capital and identifying undervalued assets with strong recovery potential. Adapting to these cycles ensures the portfolio remains resilient and well-positioned for future growth.

Taking profits in a volatile market is both an art and a science. While the allure of holding onto investments for even greater returns is tempting, it's essential to recognize that no market rises indefinitely. Profit-taking involves:

-Selling a portion of holdings when they have appreciated significantly.

-Locking in gains.

-Reducing exposure to potential downturns.

This practice protects the portfolio from overexposure to a single asset and provides liquidity for reinvestment or other financial goals.

One common approach to profit-taking is to sell incrementally as an altcoin's price rises. By selling in stages, investors avoid the challenge of timing the market perfectly and reduce the risk of selling too early or too late. For instance, if an altcoin doubles in value, selling a portion of the holding allows the investor to recover the initial investment while leaving the remaining portion to benefit from potential upside.

Profit-taking also provides an opportunity to rebalance the portfolio. As certain altcoins outperform and grow disproportionately within the portfolio, their increased weight can shift the overall risk profile. Selling a portion of these high-performing assets and reallocating the proceeds to underweighted or undervalued assets restores balance and aligns the portfolio with the investor's original strategy. Rebalancing in this way helps manage risk and maintain diversification, ensuring that the portfolio remains robust against market fluctuations.

Emotional discipline is critical when taking profits in a volatile market. The fear of missing out (FOMO) can lead to holding onto investments longer than necessary, while the fear of a market reversal may prompt premature selling. Setting clear profit targets and adhering to them reduces the influence of emotions, enabling investors to act decisively and consistently. For example, an investor might decide to take profits once an altcoin's price increases by 50% or reaches a specific milestone. Having predefined criteria for profit-taking ensures that decisions are based on strategy rather than impulse.

Exiting poor-performing altcoins is equally important for maintaining a healthy portfolio. Not all investments will succeed, and recognizing when to cut losses is crucial for any investor. Holding onto underperforming assets in the hope of a turnaround can lead to further losses and missed opportunities elsewhere. Exiting these positions allows investors to reallocate capital to more promising ventures and optimize the portfolio's overall performance.

Determining when to exit a poor-performing altcoin requires objective analysis and practical judgment. One common indicator is a consistent price or trading volume decline, which may signal waning interest or market confidence. However, price alone is not always sufficient to justify an exit. Understanding the reasons behind the decline is key. For instance, a temporary dip due to broader market conditions might not warrant immediate action. At the same time, a prolonged downturn caused by fundamental issues within the project could indicate a deeper problem.

Assessing the health of a project's fundamentals is a critical step in deciding whether to exit. Warning signs such as a lack of development activity, unresolved technical issues, or negative news about the team or partnerships should not be ignored. For example, if a project repeatedly fails to meet its roadmap milestones or faces allegations of fraud or mismanagement, these are strong indications that the investment is at risk. In such cases, exiting the position early can prevent further losses and free up resources for more promising opportunities.

Investor sentiment and community engagement also play a role in evaluating poor-performing altcoins. Projects with active and supportive communities often have a higher chance of recovery, as the collective effort and enthusiasm can drive renewed interest and development. Conversely, projects that lose community trust or engagement may need help to regain traction, making them less viable long-term investments. Monitoring sentiment through social media platforms, forums, and project updates provides valuable context for exit decisions.

The psychological aspects of exiting poor-performing altcoins must be considered. The sunk cost fallacy, where investors hesitate to sell because of the time or money already invested, is a common barrier to cutting losses. Overcoming this mindset requires focusing on the potential future performance of the asset rather than its past. Accepting losses as a natural part of investing and prioritizing the portfolio's overall health enables investors to make more rational decisions.

Rebalancing and exit strategies are essential for navigating the dynamic and unpredictable world of altcoin investments. Investors can manage risk, preserve capital, and optimize returns by regularly reassessing investments, taking profits strategically, and exiting poor-performing assets. These practices ensure the portfolio remains aligned with market conditions and individual goals, providing a strong foundation for long-term success in the ever-evolving cryptocurrency landscape.

# CHAPTER 13: COMMUNITY AND DEVELOPER ECOSYSTEMS

*"The strength of a community is measured by its willingness to support each other."* — *Vitalik Buterin.*

Buterin's observation highlights the central role of the community in the success of altcoin projects. Unlike traditional companies with centralized decision-making structures, altcoins rely on decentralized ecosystems where community engagement drives innovation, adoption, and sustainability. A strong community can differentiate between an altcoin that thrives and fades into obscurity.

Developers, users, and advocates form the backbone of an altcoin ecosystem. Developers contribute to the project's technical progress, ensuring that it remains relevant and competitive. Users drive adoption by participating in the network and spreading awareness. Advocates amplify the project's message, fostering a sense of belonging and shared purpose. Community-led governance models, such as those employed by decentralized autonomous organizations (DAOs), further emphasize the importance of collaboration. By giving stakeholders a voice in decision-making, these models create transparency and accountability, aligning the interests of all participants.

Buterin's insight reminds us that community is not just an asset but a driving force behind altcoin success. In the blockchain space, where trust and participation are paramount, the strength of a community can determine a project's trajectory. Engaged and supportive communities are the lifeblood of altcoins, fueling innovation and ensuring their long-term viability.

The strength of a cryptocurrency project often lies in its unique features, such as the community and developer ecosystem. These ecosystems, unlike traditional financial systems, are the lifeblood of altcoins and drive growth, adoption, and innovation. Blockchain projects thrive on decentralized users, developers, and advocates networks. Communities foster trust and engagement, developers contribute to technical progress, and crowdsourcing empowers real-world applications. Together, these elements shape the trajectory of altcoins in a dynamic and competitive landscape.

The role of the community in altcoin growth cannot be overstated. Communities are not just the backbone of a project, but also the driving force, providing the energy and enthusiasm necessary to sustain momentum. Whether through social media, forums, or in-person events, community members amplify a project's message, rally support during challenging times, and advocate for its adoption. Their contributions are not just appreciated, but integral to the project's success. A strong community can often differentiate between an altcoin that thrives and one that fades into obscurity, and this is a testament to their empowerment and value.

In cryptocurrency, a project's community is not just a marketing tool, but a family. Enthusiastic supporters generate organic buzz by sharing updates, creating content, and engaging with potential users or investors. These efforts build awareness and credibility, especially for new or emerging projects. Platforms like Twitter, Reddit, and Telegram have become hubs where communities form and flourish, fostering conversations about the potential and progress of specific altcoins. When a community believes in a project's vision and values, it's not just about inspiring others to take notice and join the movement, but about creating a sense of belonging and connection.

Building trust and adoption is one of the most critical functions of a community. Trust is the foundation upon which any successful project rests, and in the world of decentralized finance, where anonymity and volatility are prevalent, establishing trust is particularly challenging. Communities play a pivotal role in bridging this gap by demonstrating genuine engagement, transparency, and commitment to the project's mission. When users see a vibrant, active community invested in the project's success, they are more likely to trust its longevity and potential.

Trust-building often begins with transparency, a key factor in the success of cryptocurrency projects. Projects that share regular updates acknowledge challenges and celebrate milestones foster a sense of accountability. Communities amplify these efforts by holding projects to high standards, ensuring developers and leaders remain true to their promises. This dynamic creates a positive feedback loop, where transparency builds trust, and trust drives adoption.

Adoption is another area where communities have a profound impact. Altcoins that gain traction often do so because their communities champion use cases and advocate for integration into everyday life. Whether promoting a token for payments, encouraging staking, or highlighting innovative applications, communities are instrumental in expanding an altcoin's reach. When their efforts bear fruit and their altcoin gains traction, it's not just about expanding the altcoin's reach, but about a sense of pride and achievement that motivates them to continue their advocacy.

Developers form the technical core of any altcoin ecosystem, translating ideas into functional code and applications. Blockchain technology's decentralized and open-source nature means that developer contributions are often voluntary, driven by passion, curiosity, and a belief in the project's potential. Open-source contributions are a hallmark of successful blockchain projects, enabling collaboration and innovation at an unprecedented scale.

The open-source model allows developers worldwide to contribute to a project, improving its functionality, security, and scalability. This approach fosters diversity of thought and expertise as developers bring unique perspectives and skills. Open-source ecosystems encourage transparency, as anyone can review the code, identify vulnerabilities, or suggest enhancements. This openness builds confidence in the project's technical integrity and ensures it evolves in response to user needs and market demands.

One notable example of the power of open-source contributions is Ethereum. As the second-largest cryptocurrency by market capitalization, Ethereum has become a hub for developer activity, with countless dApps, protocols, and tools built on its blockchain. Its open-source framework has enabled developers worldwide to innovate and experiment, driving the growth of decentralized finance, non-fungible tokens, and other blockchain-based industries. This collaborative ecosystem underscores the value of open-source development in accelerating progress and adoption.

Beyond code, developers also play a critical role in educating and empowering communities. Many blockchain projects host developer tutorials, workshops, and documentation to lower the barriers to entry for newcomers. By creating resources that demystify complex concepts and provide step-by-step guidance, developers enable more individuals to participate in the ecosystem. This inclusivity not only broadens the talent pool but also strengthens the project's resilience and adaptability.

Real-world applications through crowdsourcing highlight the intersection of community and developer ecosystems. Crowdsourcing leverages a project's supporters' collective creativity and expertise to solve problems, generate ideas, and create new use cases. This approach embodies the decentralized ethos of blockchain technology, empowering individuals to contribute meaningfully to a project's growth and success.

Blockchain-based crowdfunding platforms, such as Gitcoin, illustrate the potential of crowdsourcing. Gitcoin connects developers with funding opportunities for open-source projects, enabling them to work on initiatives that align with their skills and passions. This model not only supports innovation but also reinforces the collaborative nature of blockchain ecosystems. Through crowdsourcing, projects can tackle challenges ranging from scalability and security to user experience and accessibility.

The impact of crowdsourcing extends beyond technical development. Community-driven initiatives often identify new applications for blockchain technology, expanding its relevance and reach. For example, decentralized autonomous organizations (DAOs) exemplify how crowdsourcing can enable collective decision-making and resource allocation.

DAOs rely on token holders to propose and vote on initiatives, ensuring that the community's voice shapes the project's direction. This participatory model has been used to fund charitable efforts, govern protocols, and support creative endeavors, demonstrating the versatility of blockchain-based crowdsourcing.

The interplay between community and developer ecosystems is a defining feature of successful altcoins. Communities provide the passion and advocacy needed to drive adoption, while developers supply the technical expertise that brings ideas to life. Together, they create a dynamic and resilient ecosystem capable of weathering challenges and seizing opportunities. As the cryptocurrency market continues to evolve, the importance of these ecosystems will only grow, shaping the future of decentralized technology and innovation.

## Developer Activity As A Key Metric

In the world of altcoins, developer activity is one of the most telling indicators of a project's health, growth potential, and sustainability. Unlike traditional markets, where financial performance or corporate revenues may dominate evaluations, the decentralized nature of blockchain technology places a premium on ongoing innovation and technical progress. Developer activity reflects a project's capacity to adapt, innovate, and deliver on its promises, making it a vital metric for investors, users, and stakeholders. By examining GitHub activity, analyzing partnerships and grants, and understanding ecosystem growth strategies, it becomes clear why developer involvement is crucial in evaluating the long-term potential of altcoins.

GitHub activity serves as a window into the technical heartbeat of a project. GitHub, a widely used platform for hosting open-source code, provides a transparent view of how actively developers contribute to a blockchain project. Metrics such as the number of commits, code changes, pull requests, and issues resolved can reveal the intensity of development and the project's focus on innovation. High activity levels suggest that a project is not stagnant but is actively improving, fixing bugs, and introducing new features. Conversely, a lack of activity can raise concerns about whether the project has stalled or is being deprioritized.

Regular updates on GitHub also indicate that a project responds to user feedback and addresses challenges as they arise. For example, if users report security vulnerabilities or request new features, timely code updates demonstrate a commitment to the community and the ecosystem's growth. Ethereum, one of the most active blockchain projects on GitHub, exemplifies how consistent developer engagement drives progress. Its open-source nature and developer-first approach have enabled a robust ecosystem of decentralized applications, DeFi protocols, and innovative tools to flourish.

However, evaluating GitHub activity requires nuance. Not all projects publish their code on GitHub; some may use private repositories or alternative platforms. Additionally, raw activity metrics alone do not guarantee quality or relevance. It is essential to assess the substance of contributions, such as the complexity of changes or the implementation of key features outlined in the project's roadmap. Investors and stakeholders should consider the context of GitHub activity alongside other indicators of project health.

Partnerships and grants are another important dimension of developer activity. Strategic partnerships with established organizations, universities, or other blockchain projects often bring additional resources, credibility, and technical expertise to an altcoin ecosystem. When a project collaborates with major players in the industry, it signals a level of trust and recognition that can attract further developer interest and investment.

Grants from the project's treasury, external foundations, or industry initiatives provide vital funding for developers to contribute to the ecosystem. Many blockchain projects allocate grants to incentivize the development of decentralized applications, tools, or infrastructure that expand the project's utility. For instance, Polkadot's Web3 Foundation has awarded grants to numerous teams working on parachains, wallets, and interoperability solutions, significantly enhancing its ecosystem.

Partnerships and grants also foster innovation by creating opportunities for collaboration and experimentation. For example, partnerships with academic institutions can enable cutting-edge blockchain scalability, privacy, or governance research. Similarly, grants can empower independent developers to tackle niche challenges or explore novel use cases that the team has yet to prioritize. These efforts collectively contribute to the project's resilience and adaptability, ensuring it remains relevant in a rapidly evolving market.

Ecosystem growth strategies are closely linked to developer activity, as they reflect a project's broader vision for attracting talent, fostering collaboration, and expanding its reach. Successful altcoins often employ proactive strategies to engage developers and encourage contributions. These strategies may include hosting hackathons, offering bounties, or establishing incubator programs to support new projects built on their platforms. Such initiatives cultivate innovation and create a network effect, where the growing number of developers and projects enhances the overall value of the ecosystem.

Developer-friendly tools and documentation are a cornerstone of ecosystem growth. Projects that prioritize accessibility and usability for developers attract a broader pool of talent, including newcomers to blockchain development. Clear and comprehensive documentation, tutorials, and development kits lower the barriers to entry, enabling more individuals to build and experiment within the ecosystem. For example, the Solana blockchain has invested heavily in providing developers with resources, including grants, tutorials, and technical support. This has led to a surge in dApps and tools built on its platform.

Community engagement also plays a critical role in ecosystem growth. Active communication channels, such as Discord servers or Reddit forums, foster collaboration and knowledge-sharing among developers. Projects build a sense of belonging and purpose that drives sustained contributions by creating spaces where developers can ask questions, share insights, and discuss challenges. Developer conferences, meetups, and workshops further strengthen these connections, providing opportunities for networking, learning, and collaboration.

Ecosystem growth strategies often include initiatives to address specific challenges or capitalize on emerging trends. For example, as interoperability becomes increasingly crucial in blockchain, projects like Cosmos and Polkadot have focused on developing tools and frameworks to facilitate cross-chain communication. These efforts not only enhance the functionality of the core network but also attract developers interested in solving real-world problems. Similarly, projects prioritizing sustainability or scalability can position themselves as leaders in addressing industry-wide concerns, attracting developers aligned with those goals.

The interplay between developer activity, partnerships, and ecosystem growth ultimately determines an altcoin's trajectory. A vibrant developer ecosystem creates a virtuous cycle where contributions lead to new features, improved functionality, and increased adoption. This, in turn, attracts more developers, investors, and users, reinforcing the project's position in the market. Conversely, a lack of developer activity or strategic direction can signal stagnation, eroding confidence and value over time.

Developer activity is not merely a metric; it reflects a project's ability to innovate, adapt, and thrive. Investors and stakeholders can gain valuable insights into an altcoin's potential by evaluating GitHub activity, analyzing partnerships and grants, and understanding ecosystem growth strategies. As blockchain technology continues to evolve, developers' roles will remain central to shaping the future of decentralized systems, making their contributions indispensable to evaluating and supporting altcoin projects.

## Case Studies in Community-Led Success

The most successful blockchain projects demonstrate the power of community-led initiatives in shaping their ecosystems. Ethereum, Cardano, and Solana provide compelling case studies of how active participation, decentralized governance, and rapid ecosystem development can drive innovation and adoption. These projects highlight how community involvement and collaboration can turn ambitious ideas into thriving realities, fostering resilience, growth, and global impact.

**Ethereum's Evolutionary Improvement Proposal (EIP)** process exemplifies the effectiveness of community-led development. Ethereum was designed to be an open and collaborative platform from its inception, inviting developers, stakeholders, and users to contribute to its evolution. The EIP process formalizes this collaboration, enabling the community to propose, discuss, and implement changes to the Ethereum network. Each proposal undergoes rigorous scrutiny and debate, ensuring that changes are aligned with the platform's technical goals and broader community interests.

The EIP process has facilitated some of Ethereum's most significant advancements, such as the transition to Ethereum 2.0 and the adoption of the London Hard

Fork, which introduced the EIP-1559 fee structure. These upgrades were not dictated by a central authority but emerged through consensus-building and active participation. Developers, miners, and users engaged in extensive discussions, weighing the trade-offs of each proposal and reaching agreements that reflected the collective vision of the Ethereum community.

This collaborative approach has allowed Ethereum to adapt to the demands of a rapidly changing blockchain landscape. For example, EIP-1559 addressed long-standing concerns about network congestion and unpredictable transaction fees, enhancing the user experience and strengthening Ethereum's position as a leading platform for decentralized applications. The success of this upgrade underscores the value of community involvement in identifying pain points, proposing solutions, and driving innovation.

Ethereum's EIP process fosters transparency and inclusivity, as all proposals and discussions are publicly accessible. This openness builds trust among participants and encourages diverse contributions from developers worldwide. The process's decentralized nature ensures that no single entity has disproportionate influence, aligning with Ethereum's core principles of decentralization and accessibility.

Cardano's decentralized governance model provides another compelling example of community-led success. While many blockchain projects struggle to balance decentralization with effective decision-making, Cardano has made governance a central pillar of its ecosystem. Through its Voltaire era, Cardano introduced mechanisms for community-driven governance, empowering stakeholders to shape the network's development and direction.

**Cardano's governance model** is at the heart of its treasury system, which allocates funds to proposals that advance the ecosystem. Community members submit ideas for improvements, innovations, or initiatives, and ADA holders vote on which proposals should receive funding. This democratic process ensures that resources are directed toward projects that align with the community's priorities and vision.

Cardano's governance framework also incorporates a focus on sustainability. By linking funding to stakeholder consensus, the platform creates a self-sustaining ecosystem where resources are continually reinvested in growth and innovation. This approach contrasts with traditional corporate models, where decision-making is often concentrated among a few executives or shareholders. Cardano's decentralized governance ensures that the entire community has a voice, fostering a sense of ownership and accountability.

The success of this model is evident in the vibrant ecosystem of projects and initiatives that have emerged within Cardano. From DeFi protocols to social impact projects, the community has driven the development of diverse use cases that leverage Cardano's scalable and secure infrastructure. This growth has been accompanied by a strong emphasis on research and peer-reviewed development, ensuring that innovations are underpinned by rigorous academic standards.

Cardano's governance model also addresses

adaptability, one of the blockchain industry's most pressing challenges. The platform can respond dynamically to evolving market demands and technological advancements by empowering the community to propose and vote on changes. This flexibility positions Cardano as a resilient and forward-looking blockchain capable of navigating the complexities of a decentralized world.

**Solana's rapid ecosystem expansion** illustrates how community-driven development can achieve remarkable growth quickly. Launched in 2020, Solana promptly established itself as a high-performance blockchain platform capable of processing thousands of transactions per second. Its scalability, low fees, and developer-friendly tools attracted a wave of projects and contributors, transforming Solana into one of the most vibrant ecosystems in the blockchain space.

A key driver of Solana's success has been its focus on engaging and supporting developers. The platform offers a comprehensive suite of resources, including developer documentation, tutorials, and grants, to lower the barriers to entry and empower creators to build on its network. This commitment to developer enablement has fostered a thriving community of builders who have launched various applications, from decentralized finance to gaming and NFTs.

Hackathons have played a pivotal role in Solana's ecosystem growth, providing opportunities for developers to experiment, collaborate, and showcase their innovations. These events have attracted participants worldwide, generating a surge of creativity and talent. Many successful projects, such as Phantom

Wallet and Serum, emerged from Solana hackathons, demonstrating the value of community-driven initiatives in accelerating ecosystem development.

Solana's active engagement with its community extends beyond developers to include users, investors, and other stakeholders. The platform's emphasis on accessibility and user experience has contributed to its widespread adoption, with projects leveraging Solana's high throughput and low costs to attract millions of users. This network effect has created a virtuous cycle where the growing user base attracts more developers, which drives further adoption and innovation.

The Solana Foundation has also played a central role in fostering ecosystem growth, providing funding, support, and strategic guidance to projects building on the network. This collaborative approach has created a sense of shared purpose and momentum, uniting the community around the goal of scaling blockchain technology to new heights. Solana's rapid rise highlights the importance of aligning technical capabilities with community engagement, creating an environment where innovation can flourish.

The Ethereum, Cardano, and Solana case studies underscore the transformative power of community-led initiatives in the blockchain space. Whether through collaborative development processes, decentralized governance, or rapid ecosystem expansion, these projects demonstrate how active participation, and shared vision can drive success. As the blockchain industry continues to evolve, the lessons from these communities will serve as blueprints for future innovation, shaping the next generation of decentralized systems.

# CHAPTER 14: PREDICTING THE FUTURE OF ALTCOINS

*"If crypto succeeds, it's not because it empowers better people. It's because it empowers better institutions." — Vitalik Buterin.*

Buterin highlights the profound potential of cryptocurrencies and altcoins to reform institutions rather than focusing solely on individual gains. This perspective underscores the role of altcoins in building systems that prioritize transparency, inclusivity, and efficiency—attributes often lacking in traditional institutions. Altcoins are not just tools for individual profit but frameworks for improving how people interact with economic, governance, and technological structures.

Buterin's statement resonates strongly with the direction of many altcoins, such as those driving decentralized finance (DeFi), decentralized governance, and green initiatives. These projects are designed to challenge and ultimately enhance the effectiveness of existing institutions. By removing intermediaries, increasing accountability, and fostering broader participation, altcoins empower systems that work for the collective good. For instance, DeFi platforms open financial services to underserved populations, while governance tokens create democratic decision-making processes within digital ecosystems.

The future of altcoins lies in their ability to address global challenges like inequality, inefficiency, and lack of trust in centralized systems. Buterin's vision suggests that the success of crypto is not about a few individuals capitalizing on its potential but about reshaping the systems that govern society. This makes altcoins a critical force in the ongoing evolution of digital economies, showcasing how blockchain innovation can create better institutions and, consequently, a better world.

Raoul Pal, CEO of Real Vision and a former Goldman Sachs executive has shared his optimistic insights into the potential of altcoins within the cryptocurrency market. In November 2024, Pal expressed a bullish outlook on Solana (SOL), stating, "There couldn't be a more bullish long-term chart... When it breaks higher, it's going to accelerate." His positive outlook reflects the promising future of altcoins in the cryptocurrency market. Pal has also highlighted the significance of the Ethereum-to-Bitcoin (ETH/BTC) chart, describing it as "the most important chart in digital asset markets right now." These statements reflect a perspective on the evolving dynamics of altcoins and their roles in the broader cryptocurrency ecosystem.

As the blockchain industry evolves, the future of altcoins holds exciting opportunities and formidable challenges. Emerging trends, growth in specific sectors, expansion into new industries, and integration of artificial intelligence into blockchain development will shape how altcoins adapt and thrive in the years ahead. The potential of these decentralized systems to disrupt traditional industries and create entirely new ones is vast, but realizing that potential requires navigating the complexities of innovation, regulation, and adoption.

Emerging trends in altcoin development and adoption are already reshaping the landscape. One of the most significant trends is the rise of cross-chain interoperability. As the number of blockchain networks continues to grow, the ability to seamlessly transfer assets and data between them has become a priority. Interoperability solutions, such as Polkadot's parachains and Cosmos' inter-blockchain communication protocol, are laying the groundwork for a multi-chain future. This trend will likely lead to a more connected ecosystem where altcoins can collaborate rather than compete, fostering innovation and reducing fragmentation.

Another key trend is the increasing emphasis on environmental sustainability. The energy-intensive nature of proof-of-work blockchains, epitomized by Bitcoin, has drawn criticism and spurred the search for greener alternatives. Altcoins like Algorand and Cardano have taken proactive steps to minimize their environmental impact, positioning themselves as leaders in sustainable blockchain technology. As climate concerns grow, sustainability will become an even more critical factor in determining the success and adoption of altcoins.

The growth of specific sectors, such as decentralized finance (DeFi) and the metaverse, underscores the transformative potential of altcoins. DeFi has revolutionized traditional financial systems by offering decentralized lending, borrowing, trading, and yield-generation platforms. The rise of DeFi altcoins like Aave, Uniswap, and MakerDAO reflects the demand for financial systems that are more inclusive, transparent, and efficient. As DeFi matures, its impact will likely expand, integrating with traditional finance and attracting institutional participation.

The metaverse, an immersive digital environment where users interact through avatars and virtual assets, represents another area of rapid growth. Altcoins like Decentraland and The Sandbox are at the forefront of this movement, enabling users to own, trade, and create digital assets within virtual worlds. Integrating non-fungible tokens (NFTs) with the metaverse has further enhanced its appeal, allowing for unique ownership of virtual goods, art, and real estate. The metaverse's potential extends beyond gaming and entertainment, offering education, commerce, and social interaction opportunities.

Expansion into new industries is a natural progression as blockchain technology matures. Supply chain management, healthcare, real estate, and energy are among the sectors poised for disruption. Altcoins are increasingly used to enhance transparency, efficiency, and security in these industries, inspiring a new wave of innovation. For instance, VeChain has gained traction in supply chain management by enabling real-time tracking and verifying goods, reducing fraud and inefficiencies. In healthcare, projects like MediBloc aim to create secure and decentralized systems for managing patient data and empowering individuals while ensuring privacy.

The real estate industry is also beginning to explore blockchain's potential, with altcoins enabling fractional ownership, tokenized real estate assets, and streamlined property transactions. These innovations could democratize access to real estate investment, making it more inclusive and liquid. In the energy sector, blockchain-based solutions facilitate peer-to-peer energy trading and incentivize renewable energy adoption through tokenized rewards.

The integration of artificial intelligence (AI) with blockchain technology represents one of the most intriguing and exciting developments on the horizon. AI has the potential to enhance blockchain systems in several ways, from improving scalability and efficiency to enabling more sophisticated smart contracts. Combining AI and blockchain can also unlock new use cases, such as predictive analytics for DeFi markets, automated governance in decentralized autonomous organizations (DAOs), and intelligent routing in supply chain networks.

AI-powered analytics tools are already being used to gain insights into blockchain data, identifying patterns and trends that would be difficult for humans to discern. For example, AI can analyze transaction histories to detect fraud, optimize trading strategies, or assess the health of blockchain ecosystems. This capability has significant implications for investors, developers, and regulators, providing a deeper understanding of market dynamics and project performance.

In the realm of smart contracts, AI could enable more adaptive and intelligent automation. Traditional smart contracts operate based on predefined conditions, but integrating AI could allow for contracts that learn and adapt over time. For instance, an AI-enhanced smart contract could analyze market conditions or user behavior to optimize execution, making decentralized applications more responsive and efficient.

Decentralized governance is another area where AI could transform society. Many blockchain projects rely on community voting to make decisions, but this process can be slow and susceptible to manipulation. AI could streamline governance by analyzing proposals, evaluating their potential impact, and providing data-driven recommendations. This approach could enhance the decision-making process while preserving decentralization and community participation.

As blockchain technology expands into new domains, the ethical and regulatory implications of integrating AI must also be considered. Ensuring transparency, fairness, and accountability in AI-driven blockchain systems will build trust and foster adoption. Collaborative efforts between technologists, policymakers, and communities will be essential to address these challenges and unlock AI's full potential in the blockchain space.

The future of altcoins will likely be defined by a combination of emerging trends, sector-specific growth, industry expansion, and technological integration. As blockchain ecosystems become more interconnected and diverse, altcoins will play an increasingly central role in driving innovation and creating new economic opportunities. By embracing sustainability, interoperability, and advanced technologies like AI, altcoins can continue to disrupt traditional systems. For instance, they can revolutionize financial systems, democratize access to investment opportunities, and incentivize sustainable practices. This disruptive potential pave the way for a decentralized and inclusive future. The journey ahead promises to be as transformative as it is unpredictable, with altcoins at the forefront of a new era of digital evolution.

## Technological Innovations On The Horizon

As the blockchain industry matures, the pursuit of technological innovation remains relentless. To stay competitive and relevant, altcoins must adopt and advance new technologies that address scalability, interoperability, and privacy concerns. Emerging solutions such as advanced layer-2 scaling mechanisms, interoperability frameworks between blockchains, and zero-knowledge proof applications are set to revolutionize the altcoin ecosystem, making these networks more efficient, interconnected, and secure.

Advanced layer-2 solutions are at the forefront of addressing one of blockchain's most persistent challenges: scalability. The underlying architecture of most blockchains prioritizes decentralization and security, often at the expense of transaction throughput and speed. This trade-off has created bottlenecks, particularly during periods of high demand, leading to congestion and soaring transaction fees. Layer-2 solutions offer a promising pathway to alleviate these issues by enabling transactions to be processed off the main chain while retaining the security guarantees of the underlying blockchain.

Among the most notable advancements in layer-2 technology are rollups, including optimistic and zero-knowledge (zk) rollups. Optimistic rollups assume that transactions are valid unless challenged, significantly reducing computational requirements. In contrast, zk-rollups generate cryptographic proofs to verify the correctness of transactions, offering enhanced security and efficiency. Both approaches have gained traction within ecosystems like Ethereum, where they are helping to reduce fees and increase transaction throughput without compromising security.

Deploying layer-2 solutions transforms the user experience for altcoins by making them more accessible and affordable. For example, projects leveraging zk-rollups can process thousands of transactions per second while maintaining low fees, enabling seamless interactions for decentralized finance (DeFi) applications, gaming, and non-fungible tokens (NFTs). The ability to handle large volumes of transactions opens doors for mainstream adoption, where users expect fast and cost-effective solutions.

Interoperability between blockchains is another area poised to drive significant innovation. The proliferation of blockchain networks has created a fragmented ecosystem where assets and data are siloed within individual chains. This lack of connectivity limits the potential of blockchain technology and creates inefficiencies for users and developers alike. Interoperability frameworks aim to bridge these gaps, enabling seamless communication and interaction across blockchain networks.

Projects like Polkadot and Cosmos lead the charge in interoperability by providing frameworks that facilitate cross-chain communication. Polkadot's parachains and Cosmos' Inter-Blockchain Communication (IBC) protocol are designed to enable independent blockchains to share information and assets securely. These solutions empower developers to build applications that leverage the strengths of multiple blockchains, creating new opportunities for innovation and collaboration.

The benefits of interoperability extend beyond technical efficiency, including enhanced user experiences and expanded market opportunities. For instance, an interoperable DeFi ecosystem allows users to access liquidity and services across multiple platforms without intermediaries or manual asset transfers. Similarly, NFT marketplaces can benefit from interoperability by enabling cross-chain trading and aggregation, increasing the reach and value of digital assets.

Interoperability also fosters a sense of unity within the blockchain industry, reducing competition between chains and encouraging collaboration. By creating a more interconnected ecosystem, altcoins can collectively strengthen their position in the broader market, attracting developers, users, and investors to a cohesive and synergistic environment.

Zero-knowledge proof (ZKP) applications represent a groundbreaking innovation in privacy and security for blockchain technology. ZKPs enable one party to prove the validity of a statement to another party without revealing the underlying information. This cryptographic technique has profound implications for preserving privacy while maintaining transparency, a duality often difficult to achieve in blockchain systems.

One of the most promising applications of ZKPs is in enhancing transaction privacy. While blockchains like Bitcoin and Ethereum provide transparency by recording all transactions on a public ledger, this transparency can be a double-edged sword, exposing user data and compromising privacy. Zero-knowledge proofs allow for transactions to be verified without disclosing details such as amounts, sender, or receiver, addressing privacy concerns without sacrificing security. Privacy-focused altcoins like Zcash have already implemented ZKPs to protect user identities and transaction data, setting a precedent for broader adoption.

Beyond privacy, ZKPs have the potential to transform identity verification and authentication. Using ZKPs, individuals can prove their identity or qualifications without revealing sensitive information. For example, a person could verify their age to access age-restricted services without disclosing their date of birth or other personal details. This capability has applications in finance, healthcare, and beyond, enabling secure and privacy-preserving interactions in a digital age.

ZKPs are also being explored to improve scalability and efficiency in blockchain networks. By enabling concise proofs of computation, ZKPs reduce the amount of data that needs to be processed and stored on-chain. This optimization can significantly enhance the performance of blockchain systems, particularly as they scale to accommodate more users and use cases.

Another area of potential innovation is the integration of ZKPs into governance processes. Many blockchain projects rely on community voting for decision-making, but this process often exposes voter identities and preferences. ZKPs can enable anonymous and verifiable voting, preserving privacy while ensuring transparency and fairness. This application aligns with the decentralized ethos of blockchain technology, empowering communities to participate securely and inclusively.

The convergence of advanced layer-2 solutions, interoperability frameworks, and zero-knowledge-proof applications signals a transformative era for altcoins. These innovations address fundamental challenges that have hindered blockchain adoption, making networks more scalable, interconnected, and secure. As these technologies mature, they will enhance the functionality of individual altcoins and reshape the broader blockchain ecosystem, paving the way for a more inclusive and efficient digital future. By embracing these innovations, altcoins can continue to drive progress and unlock new possibilities in the rapidly evolving world of decentralized technology.

## Shaping The Next Big Altcoin

The evolution of altcoins has shown that dominance in the cryptocurrency market is neither static nor guaranteed. As new technologies emerge and user expectations evolve, the potential for the next big altcoin to reshape the landscape grows. The factors driving future dominance, the ability to adapt to shifting market demands, and the capacity to sustain growth through continuous innovation will be critical in determining which altcoin will lead the charge in the next phase of blockchain development.

Factors for future dominance in the altcoin space are multifaceted, reflecting technical capabilities and broader market positioning. One of the most critical elements is effectively addressing real-world problems. Altcoins that succeed in solving specific pain points or inefficiencies are more likely to gain traction and attract long-term users and investors. Whether enhancing financial inclusion, streamlining supply chains, or enabling new forms of digital ownership, altcoins must offer tangible value beyond speculative investment.

Network scalability will remain a foundational factor

in shaping the next dominant altcoin. The demand for high throughput and low transaction costs has already driven significant innovation, but the next generation of altcoins will need to go further. Scalability must be achieved without sacrificing decentralization or security, addressing the long-standing blockchain trilemma. Altcoins that implement advanced solutions like sharding, rollups, or hybrid consensus mechanisms will likely lead the way, enabling them to support mass adoption across industries.

Another critical factor is user experience. As blockchain technology moves toward mainstream adoption, usability will play an increasingly significant role in determining success. Complex interfaces, slow transaction speeds, and steep learning curves can deter new users and limit adoption. The next big altcoin will prioritize intuitive design, seamless onboarding, and integration with existing technologies, creating an ecosystem accessible to technical and non-technical audiences.

Community engagement will also shape the future of altcoin dominance. A vibrant and active community provides a foundation for growth, innovation, and resilience. Altcoins that foster strong connections with their users and developers are better positioned to weather market volatility and adapt to changing circumstances. Community-led governance models, participatory development processes, and transparent communication channels are powerful tools for building trust and loyalty. The next dominant altcoin will likely leverage these dynamics to create a sense of shared purpose and collective ownership.

Adapting to market demands is essential for any altcoin aiming to maintain relevance and competitiveness. The cryptocurrency market is dynamic, influenced by macroeconomic trends, regulatory changes, and technological advancements. Altcoins that can pivot in response to these shifts while staying true to their core mission will have a distinct advantage. Flexibility in development, governance, and strategy allows projects to seize emerging opportunities and mitigate risks, ensuring longevity in a fast-paced environment.

Regulation is one area where adaptability will be particularly important. As governments and institutions continue to explore regulatory frameworks for cryptocurrencies, altcoins must navigate a complex and evolving landscape. Compliance with anti-money laundering (AML) and know-your-customer (KYC) requirements while maintaining decentralization and user privacy will be a balancing act. Altcoins that proactively engage with regulators, adopt transparent practices, and incorporate compliance-friendly features will be better positioned to thrive in regulated markets.

Societal and cultural shifts also shape market demands. For example, the growing focus on sustainability has created opportunities for altcoins that prioritize environmental responsibility. Projects that minimize their carbon footprint, support renewable energy initiatives, or enable sustainable practices through blockchain technology will resonate with environmentally conscious users and investors. Addressing these demands requires technical innovation and strategic positioning, ensuring that altcoins align with broader societal values.

The most challenging aspect of shaping the next big altcoin is sustaining growth through innovation. While initial success often comes from addressing a specific use case or leveraging a unique technology, long-term dominance requires continuous evolution. Stagnation is a risk in any industry, but it is particularly acute in the rapidly evolving blockchain world, where new projects and technologies emerge daily.

Research and development will be key to sustaining growth. The next dominant altcoin must invest in exploring cutting-edge technologies, such as quantum-resistant cryptography, artificial intelligence integration, or advanced privacy solutions. These innovations not only enhance the network's functionality but also create new opportunities for differentiation and market expansion. A commitment to R&D signals users and investors that the project is forward-looking and prepared to adapt to future challenges.

Collaboration will also play a crucial role in fostering innovation. The decentralized nature of blockchain technology creates opportunities for altcoins to partner with other projects, institutions, and industries. Collaborative efforts like interoperability initiatives, joint research projects, or cross-chain applications enable altcoins to pool resources, share expertise, and accelerate progress. These partnerships expand the reach and capabilities of altcoin ecosystems, creating a network effect that drives further growth.

Economic incentives are another lever for sustaining innovation and growth. Altcoins that design robust incentive structures for users, developers, and validators can create self-sustaining ecosystems. For example, staking rewards, developer grants, and liquidity mining programs encourage participation and engagement, ensuring the network remains active and dynamic. By aligning incentives with long-term goals, altcoins can foster a culture of collaboration and continuous improvement.

The role of governance in sustaining growth must be considered. Decentralized governance models, where community members have a direct say in decision-making, empower users and developers to shape the future of the network. These models create a sense of ownership and accountability, ensuring that decisions reflect the collective interests of the ecosystem. Transparent and inclusive governance processes also build trust and resilience, enabling altcoins to navigate challenges and opportunities with agility.

The next big altcoin will likely emerge from technical prowess, market responsiveness, and community-driven innovation. By addressing real-world problems, adapting to changing demands, and sustaining growth through continuous development, altcoins can carve out a dominant position in the cryptocurrency landscape. As the industry evolves, these qualities will define individual projects and the broader trajectory of decentralized technology, paving the way for a more inclusive and innovative digital future.

# CHAPTER 15: THE ALTCOIN INVESTOR'S PLAYBOOK

*"Patience is a key challenge for investors during bull markets, as the temptation to overtrade can lead to mistakes that undermine long-term investment strategies."* — Raoul Pal.

Raoul Pal's observation sheds light on a critical aspect of successful investing: the importance of patience, particularly in the fast-moving world of cryptocurrencies. During bull markets, when prices soar, and market sentiment is euphoric, many investors fall prey to overtrading. Driven by the fear of missing out (FOMO), they often chase short-term gains, make impulsive trades, or shift strategies prematurely. Such actions can disrupt well-thought-out plans and erode potential long-term returns.

Pal emphasizes that real investment success comes from maintaining discipline and resisting the allure of constant trading. The temptation to act on every market fluctuation can be overwhelming in the altcoin market, where volatility is high, and price swings are dramatic. However, consistently jumping in and out of investments increases the risk of poorly timed decisions and significant losses.

Patience lets investors focus on the bigger picture, letting their investments compound over time. Instead of reacting to every peak and trough, they can evaluate opportunities clearly, aligning actions with long-term goals rather than emotional impulses. Pal's insight is particularly relevant to altcoin investors, who must navigate the inherent risks of cryptocurrency and the psychological challenges posed by rapid market movements. By staying grounded and committed to a strategic approach, investors can optimize their chances of achieving meaningful and sustainable outcomes in this dynamic and unpredictable market.

As one of the most dynamic and promising sectors within the cryptocurrency ecosystem, Altcoins hold immense potential. Their disruptive capabilities, introduction of new technologies, and potential for substantial returns have attracted diverse investors. Despite the accompanying risks, this potential, from market volatility to regulatory uncertainty and the threat of scams, should be seen as an exciting opportunity. Understanding these factors is the first step in building a robust investment strategy, and with the right approach, the potential for substantial returns can be a source of optimism and hope.

One of the most critical takeaways for investors is the need to focus on fundamentals rather than hype. The cryptocurrency market is notorious for its speculative cycles, where social media buzz, influencer endorsements, or fleeting trends can drive price movements. While these factors may create short-term opportunities, they rarely align with long-term success. Successful investors prioritize projects with strong use cases, solid technical foundations, and active development communities. They look for signs of innovation, scalability, and sustainability rather than chasing quick gains.

When evaluating altcoins, a structured framework is key. This framework should consider technical, economic, and community factors. At the technical level, assessing a project's scalability, security, and usability is essential. Projects that effectively address blockchain's scalability challenges, such as handling high transaction volumes or reducing fees, are more likely to achieve widespread adoption. Similarly, robust security measures and transparent practices inspire confidence and protect against vulnerabilities.

Economic factors play a significant role in determining an altcoin's potential. Tokenomics, a term derived from 'token' and 'economics,' refers to the financial structure of a cryptocurrency and provides insights into its value proposition. Metrics such as circulating supply, inflation or deflation rates, and utility within the ecosystem influence an altcoin's long-term viability. Projects that align token supply with demand, incentivize participation, and create meaningful use cases are better positioned for growth.

Community engagement and developer activity are equally important in evaluating altcoins. A strong community fosters trust, loyalty, and advocacy, while an active developer base ensures continuous innovation and problem-solving. By assessing the vibrancy of online forums, the frequency of updates on platforms like GitHub, and the transparency of communication between project teams and their communities, investors can feel connected to the resilience and adaptability of the altcoin ecosystem. This sense of connection and involvement can be a powerful motivator in the investment journey.

Balancing opportunity and risk is the cornerstone of successful altcoin investment. The cryptocurrency market's volatility demands a disciplined approach to portfolio management. Diversification across different altcoins, sectors, and use cases helps mitigate risks while capturing opportunities. For instance, balancing investments in established projects with those in emerging sectors, such as decentralized finance (DeFi) or the metaverse, can expose growth areas without overcommitting to speculative ventures.

Risk management also involves setting clear investment goals and boundaries. Investors should determine their risk tolerance, establish profit-taking and stop-loss strategies, and avoid overexposure to any asset. Emotional decision-making, whether driven by fear or greed, often leads to suboptimal outcomes. A well-defined strategy reduces the influence of emotions and ensures consistency in decision-making, providing a sense of security and control in the often volatile cryptocurrency market.

The cryptocurrency market offers numerous lessons from success and failure stories, providing valuable insights for investors. Projects like Ethereum highlight the importance of innovation, community collaboration, and adaptability. Ethereum's success can be attributed to its pioneering approach to smart contracts, vibrant developer ecosystem, and ability to evolve through upgrades like Ethereum 2.0. Despite challenges such as network congestion and competition, these factors have positioned it as a cornerstone of the blockchain space. On the other hand, failures like BitConnect underscore the dangers of scams, overpromising, and unsustainable business models. BitConnect lured investors with promises of guaranteed returns but collapsed as a Ponzi scheme, causing significant financial losses. This cautionary tale emphasizes the need for skepticism, due diligence, and a focus on fundamentals rather than hype.

Lessons from failures also highlight the importance of resilience and adaptability. Many projects need more support due to technical challenges, regulatory hurdles, or market downturns. The ability to navigate these obstacles, learn from mistakes, and pivot effectively is a hallmark of successful altcoins. Investors should evaluate how projects respond to adversity, as this often reveals their long-term potential.

Incorporating lessons from successes and failures into an investment strategy enhances decision-making and reduces risk. Investors can draw parallels between emerging projects and established examples, identifying traits that signal potential success or red flags that warrant caution. They can refine their approach by analyzing past outcomes and position themselves for better results.

The altcoin investor's playbook is not a static set of rules but a dynamic guide that evolves with the market. Staying informed about technological advancements, regulatory developments, and market trends is essential for adapting strategies to changing conditions. Engaging with knowledgeable communities, attending industry events, and leveraging analytics tools provide valuable perspectives and insights.

Ultimately, successful altcoin investment is about balancing vision and pragmatism. While the promise of innovation and transformation is enticing, it must be tempered by a thorough understanding of risks, a focus on fundamentals, and a commitment to disciplined decision-making. The altcoin market is a landscape of opportunities and challenges, and those who navigate it with care, curiosity, and critical thinking are best positioned to succeed in this exciting and unpredictable space.

## Crafting Your Investment Strategy

A successful investment strategy in the altcoin market requires foresight, discipline, and adaptability. As one of the most dynamic and volatile asset classes, cryptocurrencies present immense opportunities and significant risks. To navigate this landscape effectively, investors must define clear goals, establish a realistic budget, stay informed about market developments, and leverage analytics to make data-driven decisions. A well-crafted strategy not only minimizes emotional decision-making but also maximizes the potential for long-term success.

Setting goals and establishing a budget are the foundation of any investment strategy. Without a clear sense of purpose, it is easy to become swayed by market noise or succumb to the fear of missing out. Goals help anchor decision-making, providing a framework for evaluating opportunities and determining whether they align with an investor's objectives. For some, the goal is to achieve significant capital appreciation over the long term, while others prioritize generating passive income through staking or liquidity provision. Some investors may seek to diversify their portfolios to reduce exposure to traditional asset classes, while others might focus on supporting innovative blockchain projects that align with their values.

Defining these goals requires a realistic assessment of risk tolerance and time horizon. Investors with a higher risk appetite may allocate more of their portfolio to speculative altcoins. At the same time, those with a lower tolerance for volatility may focus on established cryptocurrencies with a track record of stability. Similarly, individuals with a long-term investment horizon can afford to ride out market fluctuations, while those seeking short-term gains must adopt a more active trading approach. Understanding these personal factors ensures that the investment strategy is tailored to individual circumstances and preferences.

Budgeting is equally crucial, as it sets clear boundaries for how much capital an investor is willing to commit to the altcoin market. The volatile nature of cryptocurrencies necessitates a conservative approach to budgeting, particularly for newcomers. Only funds an investor can lose should be allocated to altcoin investments. Establishing this limit reduces the emotional stress of market downturns and ensures that essential financial needs remain unaffected.

Once goals and budgets are in place, staying informed becomes the next critical component of a successful strategy. The altcoin market rushes and is influenced by technological advancements, regulatory changes, macroeconomic trends, and community sentiment. These developments allow investors to identify emerging opportunities, anticipate potential risks, and make timely portfolio adjustments.

Staying informed requires engaging with reputable sources of information. News outlets, research reports, and industry blogs provide valuable insights into market trends and project developments. Social media platforms like Twitter and Reddit can offer real-time updates, though it is important to approach these channels cautiously due to the prevalence of misinformation. Participating in community forums and attending blockchain events or webinars further enriches an investor's understanding of the ecosystem and fosters connections with other market participants.

Agility is a natural extension of staying informed.

In the fast-paced altcoin market, adapting quickly to changing conditions is essential. This might involve reallocating assets in response to shifts in market sentiment, exiting positions when a project no longer aligns with investment goals, or capitalizing on new opportunities. Agility does not mean abandoning a long-term strategy at the first sign of turbulence but maintaining the flexibility to adjust tactics within the broader framework of defined objectives.

Analytics play a pivotal role in crafting and executing an investment strategy. The sheer volume of data generated by the altcoin market can be overwhelming, but advanced analytics tools provide the means to distill this information into actionable insights. These tools range from portfolio trackers that monitor asset performance to on-chain analytics platforms that reveal trends in blockchain activity. By leveraging analytics, investors can make more informed decisions and reduce reliance on intuition or speculation.

Portfolio trackers offer a centralized view of holdings, enabling investors to assess their overall performance and adjust as needed. These tools provide insights into metrics such as profit and loss, asset allocation, and historical trends. Tracking performance over time helps investors identify which strategies are working and which may need refinement. For example, if a particular altcoin consistently underperforms the broader market, analytics can highlight this discrepancy and inform decisions about rebalancing or exiting the position.

On-chain analytics take this further by providing granular data on blockchain activity. Platforms like Glassnode and Dune Analytics offer insights into metrics such as transaction volumes, wallet distributions, and developer activity. These metrics shed light on the underlying health and adoption of an altcoin, enabling investors to differentiate between projects with genuine growth potential and those driven solely by speculative hype. For instance, a spike in wallet activity might indicate increasing user adoption, while declining developer contributions could signal stagnation.

Sentiment analysis is another valuable tool for altcoin investors. It provides a snapshot of market psychology by analyzing social media activity, news coverage, and community discussions. Understanding sentiment helps investors gauge the enthusiasm or caution surrounding a particular altcoin, offering clues about potential price movements. While sentiment should not be the sole basis for investment decisions, it provides context for interpreting market behavior and aligning strategies accordingly.

Predictive analytics, powered by artificial intelligence and machine learning, represent the cutting edge of investment tools. These systems analyze historical data and identify patterns to forecast market trends, price movements, or project performance. Predictive analytics can help investors anticipate opportunities or risks, enabling them to act proactively rather than reactively. For example, an AI model might identify an impending price breakout based on trading volume patterns and order book activity, allowing an investor to position themselves accordingly.

Crafting an investment strategy also involves reflecting

on past decisions and learning from experience. Every investor, regardless of expertise, will encounter successes and failures. Analyzing these outcomes provides valuable lessons that refine strategies and enhance decision-making. For instance, reflecting on a profitable trade might reveal the importance of timing or the effectiveness of a particular analysis tool. Similarly, examining a loss might highlight the need for stricter risk management or more thorough due diligence.

Discipline is a recurring theme in successful investment strategies. Sticking to predefined goals, budgets, and decision-making criteria helps investors avoid the pitfalls of emotional reactions or impulsive behavior. This discipline includes recognizing when to take profits, cut losses, or exit positions entirely. While holding onto assets indefinitely in hopes of more significant gains can be tempting, setting clear thresholds for action ensures that decisions are guided by strategy rather than sentiment.

Crafting an altcoin investment strategy is both a science and an art. It requires a foundation of clear goals and budgeting, a commitment to staying informed and agile, and analytics to uncover opportunities and manage risks. At its core, a successful strategy aligns with an investor's unique circumstances, adapts to the dynamic nature of the market, and incorporates lessons from experience. By approaching altcoin investment with a thoughtful and disciplined mindset, investors can navigate the complexities of this evolving space and position themselves for success in the exciting world of decentralized finance and innovation.

## Looking Ahead

The world of altcoins is constantly evolving, driven by rapid technological advancements, shifting market dynamics, and the ongoing expansion of blockchain applications. The future holds opportunities and challenges for altcoins as they compete for dominance, adoption, and relevance in an increasingly crowded and innovative crypto market. To remain competitive and thrive in a decentralized world, altcoin projects must continuously adapt, innovate, and align with the demands of users, developers, and investors.

The ongoing evolution of altcoins reflects the broader trajectory of blockchain technology as it moves from its nascent stages to more mature and impactful applications. Early altcoins primarily sought to replicate or improve upon Bitcoin's model, offering variations in transaction speed, energy efficiency, or mining algorithms. As the blockchain space grew, the focus shifted toward expanding functionality, leading to the development of smart contracts, decentralized applications (dApps), and tokenized ecosystems. Ethereum's introduction of programmable innovative agreements set the stage for this transformation, demonstrating that blockchain technology could be more than a medium for value transfer—it could serve as the foundation for decentralized innovation.

The evolution of altcoins is now marked by increasing specialization. Projects no longer compete solely on technical capabilities but on their ability to address specific use cases and industries. For example, some altcoins are designed to optimize supply chain operations, while others target the healthcare or gaming sectors. This specialization allows altcoins to carve out niches and appeal to targeted audiences, fostering deeper integration into traditional industries and creating unique value propositions.

Interoperability has become a key driver of altcoin evolution, as the fragmented nature of blockchain ecosystems poses barriers to adoption and growth. Projects enabling seamless interaction between blockchains pave the way for a more interconnected crypto landscape. This evolution mirrors the early days of the internet, where interoperability standards like HTTP and TCP/IP were essential to creating a cohesive global network. Similarly, interoperability solutions like Polkadot's parachains and Cosmos' inter-blockchain communication protocol transform blockchain networks into interconnected ecosystems, unlocking new possibilities for altcoin applications and cross-chain collaboration.

As altcoins evolve, they face the challenge of staying competitive in an increasingly saturated market. The number of blockchain projects continues to grow, each vying for attention, funding, and adoption. To differentiate themselves, altcoins must deliver tangible value and demonstrate their ability to solve real-world problems. The market is no longer impressed by speculative hype or grand promises; it demands proven use cases, robust technology, and active engagement with users and developers.

Staying competitive requires a commitment to

continuous innovation. Altcoins that rest on their laurels risk being overtaken by newer, more agile competitors. Innovation can take many forms, from introducing groundbreaking technologies to refining existing features or expanding into emerging sectors. For example, projects prioritizing sustainability by adopting energy-efficient consensus mechanisms are positioning themselves as leaders in a market increasingly concerned with environmental impact. Similarly, altcoins that integrate advanced privacy features or enable seamless cross-chain transactions are addressing critical pain points and gaining a competitive edge.

User experience is another crucial factor in staying competitive. As blockchain technology becomes more mainstream, user expectations are shifting. Complex interfaces, slow transaction speeds, and high fees are no longer acceptable. Altcoins prioritizing accessibility, usability, and affordability are more likely to attract and retain users. This emphasis on user experience also extends to developers, as providing comprehensive resources, documentation, and support encourages developers to build on a particular platform, enriching its ecosystem and enhancing its appeal.

Community engagement plays a pivotal role in maintaining competitiveness. Altcoins with strong, active communities benefit from grassroots advocacy, collective problem-solving, and organic growth. Communities serve as both a support system and a feedback loop, identifying challenges, proposing solutions, and amplifying the project's message. Transparent communication, participatory governance, and a shared sense of purpose are essential for fostering loyalty and trust within these communities.

Regulation is an area where adaptability will be particularly important for staying competitive. As governments and institutions establish frameworks for cryptocurrency oversight, altcoins must navigate a complex and evolving regulatory landscape. Compliance with anti-money laundering (AML) and know-your-customer (KYC) requirements while maintaining the decentralization and privacy that attract users to blockchain technology is a delicate balancing act. Altcoins that proactively engage with regulators, adopt transparent practices, and incorporate compliance-friendly features are better positioned to thrive in regulated markets.

Thriving in a decentralized world requires altcoins to align with the principles and values that underpin blockchain technology. Decentralization is not merely a technical feature but a philosophical commitment to empowering individuals, reducing reliance on intermediaries, and fostering inclusive participation. Altcoins that embrace these principles are more likely to resonate with users and gain traction in a decentralized future.

One way to thrive is by leveraging the network effects of decentralization. As more users, developers, and applications join an altcoin ecosystem, its value and utility increase exponentially. This virtuous cycle drives adoption and creates a competitive moat, making it difficult for competitors to replicate the ecosystem's success. Projects prioritizing inclusivity, interoperability, and open collaboration are well-suited to capitalize on these network effects.

Education and outreach are also vital for thriving in a decentralized world. Blockchain technology remains complex and often needs to be understood by the general public. Altcoins that invest in educational initiatives, user-friendly tools, and accessible resources can bridge the gap between innovation and adoption. These projects can expand their user base and solidify their market position by demystifying blockchain technology and demonstrating its real-world relevance.

Decentralized governance models are another avenue for thriving in a decentralized world. These models empower communities to participate in decision-making, fostering a sense of ownership and accountability. Governance mechanisms that are transparent, inclusive, and adaptable ensure that altcoins can evolve in response to changing conditions and stakeholder needs. Projects that embrace decentralized governance are better positioned to navigate challenges, seize opportunities, and maintain alignment with their communities.

The ongoing evolution of altcoins, their ability to stay competitive, and their capacity to thrive in a decentralized world are interconnected aspects of a larger narrative. As blockchain technology continues to reshape industries, economies, and societies, altcoins will play a central role in driving innovation and creating new possibilities. By embracing adaptability, fostering collaboration, and staying true to the principles of decentralization, altcoins can chart a path toward sustained success in the ever-changing landscape of digital finance and technology. The future of altcoins is about technological advancements and empowering individuals and communities to participate meaningfully in a decentralized and inclusive digital economy.

## Altcoin Triumphs

As we wrap up this exploration of the altcoin landscape, it's impossible not to marvel at the extraordinary success stories that have defined this space. These altcoins have defied expectations, rewritten the rules, and delivered jaw-dropping returns to those bold enough to believe in their potential.

> **Solana** - Lightning-Fast Success: Solana's journey is nothing short of electrifying. Imagine spotting Solana when it traded for less than $1 in early 2020. By late 2021, its price had surged past $250, making early investors feel like they'd discovered a hidden treasure. Its secret? Unmatched speed and scalability, powering thousands of transactions per second. Solana became the darling of decentralized finance (DeFi), NFTs, and blockchain gaming, proving that technological brilliance could deliver dazzling rewards.
>
> **Dogecoin** - The People's Coin: What started as an internet joke became a global phenomenon. Dogecoin's rise is a testament to the power of fun and community and a little help from Elon Musk. Trading at fractions of a cent for years, Dogecoin reached nearly $0.70 in 2021, creating instant millionaires and unforgettable stories. But the true magic of Dogecoin lies in its culture—a playful,

inclusive community that showed the world that investing doesn't have to be all business.

**Polygon** - The Ethereum Game-Changer: Polygon burst onto the scene as a hero for Ethereum's scaling woes. Once trading at under $0.01 in its early days, Polygon climbed to over $2.80 by 2021, proving the power of solving a real problem. Developers flocked to its efficient layer-2 solutions, users loved the reduced transaction fees, and investors celebrated as their faith in Polygon was rewarded. With partnerships ranging from Meta to major DeFi protocols, Polygon became the glue binding Ethereum's expanding universe.

**Binance Coin** - A Utility Token Turned Titan: Binance Coin (BNB) began as a modest utility token, offering fee discounts on the Binance exchange. But as Binance evolved into a crypto juggernaut, so did BNB. Starting at just $0.10 during its ICO in 2017, BNB skyrocketed past $600 by 2021. Its integration into Binance's Smart Chain ecosystem cemented its place as more than a token—it became a cornerstone of decentralized applications, DeFi, and beyond.

**Axie Infinity** - Gaming the Future: Axie Infinity wasn't just a game but a revolution. Early adopters of its AXS token, priced at less than $1 in early 2021, saw it soar to over $150 by the year's end. Axie pioneered the play-to-earn model, where gamers earned real-world income by battling adorable digital creatures. The phenomenon changed lives, especially in developing countries, proving that blockchain gaming could be fun and transformative.

These stories illuminate why altcoins continue to captivate the imagination of investors and innovators alike. They represent far more than mere financial assets; they embody creativity, ambition, and the transformative promise of a decentralized future. From reshaping how we engage with gaming and scalability to redefining digital interactions, these altcoins showcase how bold ideas paired with visionary execution can revolutionize industries and profoundly impact the lives of those who embrace them. As we look ahead, the altcoin universe remains a wellspring of potential, teeming with opportunities waiting to be seized.

In this spirit of continuous evolution, the cryptocurrency landscape is brimming with emerging projects pushing boundaries and capturing attention for their groundbreaking approaches. These innovative altcoins are poised to shape the next wave of blockchain technology and adoption significantly. Some of the most promising projects on the horizon include:

**Arbitrum (ARB)**—Scaling Ethereum with Optimistic Rollups: Arbitrum's Optimistic Rollup technology enhances Ethereum's scalability and reduces transaction fees. By processing transactions off-chain and submitting them to Ethereum in batches, Arbitrum increases throughput while maintaining security. This solution has attracted numerous decentralized applications (dApps) seeking efficient operations.

**Aptos (APT)** - Delivering High-Performance

Layer-1 Solutions: Aptos is a Layer-1 blockchain designed for speed and scalability. It aims to support various applications, from DeFi to NFTs, utilizing a novel consensus mechanism and modular architecture. Its focus on developer-friendly tools and user experience positions it as a strong contender in the blockchain space.

**Optimism (OP)** - Pioneering Layer-2 Scaling for Ethereum: Optimism employs Optimistic Rollups to enhance Ethereum's scalability. Enabling faster and cheaper transactions facilitates a more accessible environment for apps and users. Its commitment to open-source development and collaboration with the Ethereum community underscores its potential for sustained growth.

**Sui (SUI)** - Innovating with Move Language and Parallel Processing: Sui introduces smart contract security and performance advancements. By adopting the Move programming language and implementing parallel transaction processing, Sui aims to reduce latency and increase throughput, making it suitable for high-demand applications.

**Injective (INJ)**—Revolutionizing Decentralized Finance: Injective is a Layer-2 protocol focused on decentralized finance (DeFi) applications. It offers a fully decentralized exchange (DEX) with cross-chain trading capabilities to provide a seamless and efficient trading experience. Its innovative approach to DeFi has garnered attention from developers and investors.

These projects exemplify the relentless innovation

driving the altcoin sector, each uniquely addressing critical challenges while contributing to the broader adoption of blockchain technology. As the cryptocurrency market continues to mature, these emerging altcoins have the potential to play pivotal roles in shaping the future of decentralized applications, financial systems, and beyond. Their growth underscores the boundless possibilities of this transformative space, inviting us to envision—and actively shape—the next chapter of the blockchain revolution.

For investors, the altcoin market presents an unparalleled combination of risk and reward, a dynamic environment where thoughtful strategies can yield significant opportunities. Navigating this volatile yet promising landscape requires clear goals, data-driven insights, and disciplined decision-making. By leveraging analytical tools, staying connected with engaged communities, and drawing lessons from triumphs and setbacks, investors can position themselves to endure and thrive.

One truth stands out: the story of altcoins still needs to be completed. It is a narrative unfolding in real time, written by developers pushing the boundaries of technology, communities driving decentralized innovation, and investors fueling the next groundbreaking ideas. Altcoins represent more than profit—they embody the potential to build a digital economy that is more open, inclusive, and creative than ever before.

This book has been your guide to understanding, evaluating, and participating in the evolving altcoin ecosystem. But ultimately, the future of this space is in your hands. Whether you approach it as an investor seeking growth, a developer driving innovation, or an enthusiast supporting transformative ideas, your decisions and actions will help define what comes next. The altcoin frontier awaits—bold, dynamic, and brimming with possibility. The time to step into this exciting future is now.

# NOTES

The story of Glauber Contessoto, popularly known as the "Doge Millionaire," has been extensively reported across reputable cryptocurrency and mainstream media platforms. CNBC Make It provides an in-depth account of Contessoto's journey to becoming a millionaire through his Dogecoin investment, detailing his initial commitment of his life savings and his decision to hold onto his gains despite market volatility (Source: CNBC Make It). The New York Times examines the cultural phenomenon of Dogecoin's rise, including the influence of high-profile endorsements like Elon Musk's tweets, which helped propel the coin's appeal to retail investors like Contessoto (Source: The New York Times). CoinDesk offers analytical insights into Dogecoin's market performance, exploring its community-driven growth and the significant role of social media platforms such as Reddit in fueling its popularity (Source: CoinDesk). Business Insider covers Contessoto's bold decision to invest his life savings in Dogecoin, his experience during the coin's dramatic price surge, and his reflections on the cryptocurrency market's volatility (Source: Business Insider). Additionally, Yahoo Finance provides detailed historical price data of Dogecoin, tracing its undervalued beginnings to its peak, which aligns with Contessoto's investment timeline and highlights the coin's explosive growth during that period (Source: Yahoo Finance).

Chapter 1 references foundational blockchain principles from Satoshi Nakamoto's Bitcoin: A Peer-to-Peer Electronic Cash System, available at https://bitcoin.org/bitcoin.pdf, which introduced decentralization and trustless systems. Gavin Wood's Polkadot Whitepaper, accessible at https://polkadot.network/Polkadot-Whitepaper.pdf, provides insights into multichain interoperability. The Avalanche platform's consensus innovations are supported by its official documentation at https://docs.avax.network/. Ethereum.org, available at https://ethereum.org/en/, is referenced for Ethereum's community-driven ecosystem and its pioneering role in smart contracts. Cardano's peer-reviewed development and Project Catalyst are explored through resources at https://www.cardano.org/. Solana's scalability solutions are drawn from its technical documentation, found at https://solana.com/, while Algorand's pure proof-of-stake model is detailed at https://www.algorand.com/.

Chapter 2 relies on the Ethereum Whitepaper by Vitalik Buterin, available at https://ethereum.org/en/whitepaper/, to explain smart contracts and programmable blockchains. Nakamoto's Bitcoin Whitepaper, accessible at https://bitcoin.org/bitcoin.pdf, is foundational for core blockchain concepts. Avalanche's documentation at https://docs.avax.network/ and Solana's developer guides at https://solana.com/ provide detailed discussions on advanced consensus mechanisms. Ethereum.org, found at https://ethereum.org/en/, offers insights into the transition to Ethereum 2.0 and its enhanced security framework. Zcash's implementation of zero-knowledge proofs is referenced through its technical documentation at https://z.cash/technology/. Cardano's governance model is supported by IOHK's resources at https://iohk.io/, showcasing decentralized decision-making.

Chapter 3 explores decentralized finance through the Ethereum Whitepaper, available at https://ethereum.org/en/whitepaper/, which introduces the foundation for smart contract-based applications. Aave's official documentation, found at https://docs.aave.com/, highlights its lending and borrowing mechanisms. Uniswap's impact on decentralized exchanges is supported by its technical resources at https://uniswap.org/. MakerDAO's innovations in stablecoin-backed lending are detailed in its whitepaper, accessible at https://makerdao.com/en/whitepaper/. Analytics from platforms like DeFi Pulse at https://defipulse.com/ and Glassnode at https://glassnode.com/ provide real-time insights into the growth and adoption of DeFi protocols.

Chapter 4 references Axie Infinity's whitepaper, available at https://whitepaper.axieinfinity.com/, which details the game's play-to-earn mechanics and economic model. Decentraland's developer documentation, accessible at https://docs.decentraland.org/, provides insights into virtual real estate and user-generated content within its metaverse. Research from DappRadar, found at https://dappradar.com/, offers analytics on blockchain gaming trends and user engagement. The Sandbox's official resources, located at https://sandbox.game/en/, discuss the integration of NFTs and the creation of virtual experiences.

Chapter 5 utilizes the Monero whitepaper, available at https://www.getmonero.org/resources/research-lab/, to explore its privacy protocols. Zcash's documentation, accessible at https://z.cash/technology/, explains its implementation of zero-knowledge proofs. The Secret Network's developer resources, found at https://docs.scrt.network/, provide information on private smart contracts. Messari's analytics, available at https://messari.io/, offer data on the adoption and market performance of privacy coins.

Chapter 6 examines Chainlink's whitepaper, accessible at https://chain.link/whitepaper, which discusses decentralized oracle networks. Filecoin's documentation, found at https://docs.filecoin.io/, details its decentralized storage solutions. Helium's technical papers, available at https://docs.helium.com/, cover its IoT applications and network architecture. Glassnode's analytics, accessible at https://glassnode.com/, provide insights into utility token metrics and network activity.

Chapter 7 references Algorand's sustainability reports, available at https://www.algorand.com/resources/blog/algorand-carbon-negative-network, highlighting its carbon-negative initiatives. Nano's official resources, found at https://docs.nano.org/, discuss its energy-efficient consensus mechanism. SolarCoin's documentation, accessible at https://solarcoin.org/, explains its approach to incentivizing renewable energy production. CoinDesk articles, available at https://www.coindesk.com/, provide context on eco-friendly blockchain projects and their environmental impact.

Chapter 8 cites CoinTelegraph's reporting on Ripple's partnerships with financial institutions, accessible at https://cointelegraph.com/tags/ripple, illustrating corporate adoption of altcoins. Deloitte's blockchain research, found at https://www2.deloitte.com/global/en/pages/consulting/solutions/blockchain.html, outlines institutional trends in blockchain technology. VeChain's technical papers, available at https://www.vechain.org/, provide use cases in supply chain management and product authentication.

Chapter 9 draws on Vitalik Buterin's Ethereum Whitepaper, accessible at https://ethereum.org/en/whitepaper/, to discuss evaluation metrics for blockchain projects. Polkadot's documentation, found at https://polkadot.network/technology/, offers insights into measuring developer activity and ecosystem development. Messari's analytics, available at https://messari.io/, support the assessment of token utility and market performance.

Chapter 10 references the World Economic Forum's reports on cryptocurrency regulation, accessible at https://www.weforum.org/agenda/archive/cryptocurrency/, providing insights into global regulatory approaches. The Financial Action Task Force's guidelines, found at https://www.fatf-gafi.org/publications/fatfrecommendations/documents/guidance-rba-virtual-assets.html, highlight compliance standards in the crypto space. CoinDesk articles, available at https://www.coindesk.com/, detail regulatory environments in crypto-friendly regions.

Chapter 11 utilizes Bloomberg's investigative reporting on BitConnect, accessible at https://www.bloomberg.com/, to illustrate the risks of fraudulent projects. Glassnode's analytics, found at https://glassnode.com/, provide data on market volatility and liquidity. Chainalysis, available at https://www.chainalysis.com/, offers insights into identifying scam patterns and technical vulnerabilities.

Chapter 12 uses CoinGecko, available at https://www.coingecko.com/, for portfolio tracking strategies. Glassnode's data, available at https://glassnode.com/, enriches risk-reward insights. Educational resources from Binance Academy, accessible at https://academy.binance.com/, provide foundational investment knowledge.

Chapter 13 references Ethereum's GitHub activity at https://github.com/ethereum and Cardano's community-driven governance in Project Catalyst, detailed at https://www.cardano.org/. LunarCrush supports social sentiment analysis at https://lunarcrush.com/.

Chapter 14 incorporates Messari and DeFi Pulse analytics at https://messari.io/ and https://defipulse.com/ to forecast sector growth. Polkadot's and Cosmos' interoperability frameworks are detailed in their whitepapers, available at https://polkadot.network/ and https://cosmos.network/. Zcash's privacy innovations are documented at https://z.cash/technology/.

Chapter 15 references Saifedean Ammous' The Bitcoin Standard, found at https://saifedean.com/book/, for economic principles relevant to crypto. CoinMarketCap at https://coinmarketcap.com/ provides real-time data for dynamic portfolio management. Blockchain trends are contextualized using reports from Deloitte at https://www2.deloitte.com/global/en/pages/consulting/solutions/blockchain.html and PwC at https://www.pwc.com/gx/en/services/legal/blockchain.html.

# INDEX

**A**

Aave
Transforming decentralized lending, 48–49
Protocol mechanics, 51
Integration with other DeFi platforms, 53

Adoption
Institutional, trends in, 201–205
Community-driven growth, 147–149
Cross-sector applications, 181–183

Altcoins
Categories, 22–23
Foundations of, 15–30
Future trends, 283–289
Interoperability between, 266–268
Role in blockchain ecosystems, 29–30

Analytics
Portfolio tracking tools, 161–163
On-chain metrics, 76, 162
Predictive models in investment, 167

Avalanche
Consensus mechanism, 17–18
Scaling capabilities, 19
Position in DeFi ecosystems, 202

## B

**Bitcoin**
Comparison with altcoins, 24–26
Role in shaping blockchain foundations, 15–16

**Blockchain Technology**
Core principles, 73–74
Layer-2 scaling solutions, 75–76
Security features, 80–83
Zero-knowledge proofs, 83–85

**Bloomberg**
Case study on BitConnect fraud, 219

**Bulldog Trading Platforms**
Emerging altcoin ecosystems, 162

## C

**Cardano**
Community initiatives (Project Catalyst), 153
Governance model, 86, 153
Role in sustainability, 138

**Chainalysis**
Tools for identifying risks, 219

**Chainlink**
Utility in oracle solutions, 136–137

**Community Engagement**
Developer contributions, 151
Governance in decentralized ecosystems, 87, 154

**Compliance**
AML and KYC requirements, 186
Strategies for balancing innovation and regulation, 186

## D

Decentraland
Virtual real estate innovations, 89–90
Integration of NFTs, 93

Decentralization
Frameworks for governance, 16, 86–87
Community impact, 149–151
Scalability challenges, 22

DeFi (Decentralized Finance)
Lending and borrowing models, 47–50
Automated market makers, 49
Growth trends, 48, 202

Diversification
Strategies for altcoin portfolios, 159–160
Balancing risks and rewards, 160–161

## E

Ethereum
Smart contracts, 74–75
EIP (Ethereum Improvement Proposals), 151
Transition to proof-of-stake, 84

Expansion
Sector-specific, 271–272
Role of institutional adoption, 201–203

## F

Filecoin
Decentralized storage solutions, 136

Frameworks
Evaluating altcoin projects, 76, 181

Fraudulent Projects
BitConnect case study, 218–219

## G
Glassnode
Data analytics for altcoin evaluation, 162, 219

Governance Coins
Role in decentralized decision-making, 147, 153

Green Blockchain Solutions
Sustainable consensus mechanisms, 138–139
Projects like Algorand and SolarCoin, 140

## H
Helium
IoT connectivity and utility, 137

Hyperledger
Blockchain interoperability examples, 268

## I
Innovation
Altcoin-driven blockchain advancements, 75–76, 271
Zero-knowledge proof applications, 85

Interoperability
Importance in blockchain ecosystems, 267

Investment Strategies
Rebalancing portfolios, 163
Balancing short-term vs. long-term goals, 159

## L
Layer-2 Solutions
Scaling mechanisms for altcoins, 75–76

LunarCrush
Social sentiment analytics, 154

**M**
MakerDAO
Stablecoin-backed lending innovation, 50

Market Trends
Institutional and community drivers, 201, 283

Metaverse
Altcoins powering virtual economies, 89

Messari
Data insights on utility tokens, 136, 154

Monero
Privacy protocols, 135

**N**
Nano
Energy-efficient transaction model, 139

NFTs (Non-Fungible Tokens)
Integration in gaming ecosystems, 93
Utility in metaverse applications, 89

**P**
Polkadot
Multichain architecture, 16, 268
Interoperability framework, 267

Privacy Coins
Use cases and challenges, 135–136

Proof-of-Stake
Energy-efficient consensus models, 84, 138

Proof-of-Work
Bitcoin's foundation, 16, 138

## S
Scalability
Challenges in blockchain adoption, 22–23
Altcoin solutions for, 19, 21

Secret Network
Private smart contracts, 136

SolarCoin
Incentives for renewable energy, 140

Solana
High-performance blockchain innovations, 19
Proof-of-History consensus, 20

## T
Tokenomics
Utility and adoption metrics, 181

Transparency
Role in decentralized governance, 154

## V
VeChain
Supply chain integration, 204

## Z
Zero-Knowledge Proofs
Applications in blockchain security, 85
Role in privacy-focused altcoins, 136

www.ingramcontent.com/pod-product-compliance
Lightning Source LLC
Chambersburg PA
CBHW071624220526
45469CB00002B/468